Letters to a
Young Journalist

Also by Samuel G. Freedman

*Small Victories: The Real World of a Teacher,
Her Students, and Their High School*

Upon This Rock: The Miracles of a Black Church

*The Inheritance: How Three Families and America
Moved from Roosevelt to Reagan and Beyond*

Jew Versus Jew: The Struggle for the Soul of American Jewry

Who She Was: My Search for My Mother's Life

www.samuelfreedman.com

Samuel G. Freedman

letters to a
young journalist

BASIC
BOOKS

A Member of the Perseus Books Group
New York

To my mentors,

Robert W. Stevens, Jim Podgers, Cissi Falligant,

Jeff Schmalz, Arthur Gelb, Abe Rosenthal, Alice Mayhew

Books published by Basic Books are available at special discounts for bulk purchases in the United States by corporations, institutions, and other organizations. For more information, please contact the Special Markets Department at the Perseus Books Group, 11 Cambridge Center, Cambridge, MA 02142, or call (617) 252–5298 or (800) 255–1514, or email special.markets@perseusbooks.com.

Set in 11-point Janson Text by the Perseus Books Group

Library of Congress Cataloging-in-Publication Data
    Freedman, Samuel G.
    Letters to a young journalist / Samuel G. Freedman.
        p. cm.
    Includes bibliographical references and index.
    ISBN–13: 978–0–465–02455–1 (alk. paper)
    ISBN–10: 0–465–02455–6 (alk. paper)
    1. Journalism. 2. Journalism—Vocational guidance. I. Title.

PN4731.F67 2006
070.4—dc22

                                              2005037974

06 07 08 09/ 10 9 8 7 6 5 4 3 2 1

■ Contents

▪ Acknowledgments

Chip Rossetti first approached me about writing this book in 2003, and he believed more firmly than I did that I was qualified to do it. I hope that the final product rewards his patient persistence. When Chip left Basic Books, Joann Miller adopted the project, and she has been an acute and engaged editor, much to my benefit. I owe a special thanks to my longtime editor, Alice Mayhew of Simon and Schuster, for allowing me this one time around the dance floor with a different partner. Now that it's over, I hope she will be editing all my work for years to come. My agent, Barney Karpfinger, has been a friend, support, and editorial adviser for twenty-one years and six books.

A number of my colleagues at the Columbia University Graduate School of Journalism provided helpful advice on readings in journalism history and ethics. I thank Nick Lemann, Sara Barrett, June Cross, Andie Tucher, John Dinges, and Sandy Padwe. Two other Columbia comrades, Michael Shapiro and Nancy Bobrowitz, who go back with me as far as the *Suburban Trib*, reminded me what made that period of our lives so special. Alice Alexiou taught me about the classical roots of narrative nonfiction, and Russell Goings offered great insights into the techniques of Romare Bearden. For fifteen years, the students of Columbia Journalism School have inspired me to make my efforts both in the classroom and on the printed page worthy of them.

Peter Edelman, researcher extraordinaire, was his usual invaluable self on this book, our fourth together. I also thank Inge De Taeye at the Karpfinger Agency and Ellen Garrison, Jason Brantley, Carol Smith, and Elizabeth Maguire at Basic Books.

Finally, I give not just an acknowledgment but all my love and gratitude to my wife, Cynthia, and my children, Aaron and Sarah, who keep me rooted.

Thirty years ago, when I was a good deal like you, I drove off to start my first job as a newspaper reporter. By that evening in May 1975, I had already been writing for student newspapers for nearly half my life, starting in junior high school. This summer internship on the *Courier-News*, a 45,000-circulation daily in suburban New Jersey, marked the first time I would actually be paid a salary for doing the thing I loved. In all the years since, I have tried never to forget the exhilaration I felt on that first night.

I was a few months short of nineteen then, and I didn't even own a white shirt or navy blazer for the occasion. If memory serves, I borrowed a leisure suit, of all things, from my father, and because he was three inches shorter than me, it couldn't have fit very well. My hair spilled down to my shoulders in coarse heaps, and I had the scraggly whiskers of a first beard, which I'd begun a few months earlier on a backpacking trip in Oregon. I must have looked like a complete buffoon.

Still, I had what was most essential to my calling, a ballpoint pen and a stenographer's notebook, and that equipment mattered more than my incompetent attire. I reached the *Courier-News* parking lot just before my shift, six thirty at night until two thirty in the morning. There was no pretense of training or orientation. I'd been hired because my clips from the college paper had convinced the editors I was capable, so I was dropped instantly into the pool of reporters covering local government. Whenever someone went on vacation, I filled in on the vacant beat. I can still remember that first night being sent to cover the township council in a place called Branchburg. I made my deadline and even slipped in the verb "assuage" in my lead paragraph, earning a sort of admiring snort from the night editor.

After I filed the story, I had my first real chance to survey the scene around me. The *Courier-News* occupied a low-slung modern building of white bricks and smoked windows, one that could have been easily mistaken for the insurance offices or furniture stores nearby on Route 22. Inside the newsroom, fluorescent lights cast a permanent daytime over banks of fake-wood desks and manual typewriters. The editors sat in a row at the front of the room with pots of rubber cement to glue together the pages of copy into a single, extended sheet for the backshop. They also had a spike for the stories that were killed. Along the wall behind the editors clattered the wire-service machines. On the far side of two swinging doors lay the composing room and presses, which were manned by burly, ink-smeared printers who thought reporters were a bunch of wimps. Down a narrow hallway was our "cafeteria," which consisted of six or seven vending machines. One of them had microwavable pancakes.

Even on my first night, I knew enough about journalism to know this wasn't the mythological world of *The Front Page*. We weren't in a city. Nobody was wearing a fedora or sneaking booze from a desk drawer or shouting things like, "Gimme rewrite, babe." The *Courier-News* once had been such a place, a fixture in the downtown of Plainfield, New Jersey, a small city that made its modest way on paychecks from a Mack Truck factory. When the black section of town had burst into rioting in 1967, with a mob stomping to death a white cop, the *Courier-News* began plotting its departure for the suburbs.

The reporters whom I got to know over the coming weeks seemed drawn in equal parts from the past and the future. There was an old-timer named Forrest who liked to avoid being assigned obituaries by hiding under his desk. One of his contemporaries, Maggie, sometimes fell asleep at her desk, letting her wig slide off. Phil, one of the editors, chewed cigars. I couldn't dismiss the whole generation, though, because it also included Jack Gill, the streetwise skeptic who covered Plainfield, and Hollis Burke, an idealist who had done a midlife turn in the Peace Corps. They had about them not only experience but wisdom.

Naturally enough, I gravitated to the younger faction, the reporters and editors in their twenties, college-educated and ambitious. Ann Devroy, the city editor, would be smoking and eating patty-melt sandwiches as she pored over copy through her tinted aviator glasses.

Sam Meddis, one of the investigative reporters, had talked his way into the paper with a bunch of poems he'd written as a Rutgers undergrad. Ultimately, Ann would become the White House correspondent for the *Washington Post*, Sam a feature writer for *USA Today*; others from that newsroom landed on the *Baltimore Sun*, *Newsday*, and *The New York Times*. That summer, though, such destinations felt impossibly distant.

It was sufficient, at least for me, to be making the lordly sum of $130 a week. I sat through a score of municipal meetings—borough council, board of education, zoning commission—and I called a half-dozen police departments for our daily roundup of local crime. Because I befriended the paper's drama critic, he let me review a few summer-stock productions. I reveled in being part of that community of reporters, sharing ziti dinners before we scattered to our various assignments, grabbing last call at the Ambers before we drove home. Those muggy Jersey nights never seemed more seductive.

Toward the end of the summer, I was subbing for the beat reporter in South Bound Brook, a blue-collar town that was uneventful even by our sleepy standards. Somebody called me with a tip, the only bona fide tip of my entire summer, that there was a suspicious pile of debris on a canal towpath that fell within the town boundary. I drove out there, probably in my leisure suit, and indeed found a pile of dirt about fifteen feet high. On closer inspection, I noticed the dirt was covering spongy, whitish material. That set off alarms for me. The asbestos manufacturer Johns Manville had its main factory a few miles away, and hundreds of its current or former employees had developed an otherwise rare cancer as a result of inhaling the dust. I wrote an initial story about my curious discovery on the towpath, which in turn brought out a scientist from the state environmental protection agency to test the pile's content. It was, sure enough, asbestos. That became my second scoop. The owner of the towpath property responded by hiring a college kid to guard the pile—by sitting on top of it in a chaise lounge. And that development, accompanied by a front-page photo, was scoop number three. Some nights, when I walked past Forrest in the newsroom, he would mutter at me, "Asbestos. You're the one. Yes, you are. With that asbestos." I was never sure whether he meant the nattering as a compliment or a condemnation. By the end of August, I'd learned it was safest to engage Forrest on the subject of Bob Marley, an improbable passion of his.

I cannot honestly say that I made up my mind to be a journalist when I wrote those asbestos articles, because I'd probably made it up as early as eighth grade, when I volunteered to be editor-in-chief of the school paper. But there was something so confirming in the experience. It made me feel that, trite as it sounds, my work could matter. It made me feel that I did belong with people like Jack Gill and Hollis Burke and Ann Devroy and Sam Meddis, that I wasn't just a pretender, a wannabe, a hanger-on.

My last shift of the summer ended much as my first one had, with filing some municipal-government story and then waiting to be released. Charlie Nutt, the night editor, was probably only seven or eight years older than me, but he had the practiced scowl of a septuagenarian.

No reporter could leave the newsroom before two thirty unless Charlie gave a "good night," and it seemed to anguish him to do so, as if shaving a few minutes off our shift might lead to the sin of sloth, as if it might endanger our eternal souls. Whenever he said, "Good night," I noticed, he said it in a stern monotone and he said it without lifting his eyes from whatever story he was editing. We would scuttle out like cockroaches. When I got my last good night of the summer, though, I was sorry to hear it, sorry to have something magical end.

I tell you this story because it never hurts to start at the beginning, and I tell you it because you've asked me for advice, and you ought to know something about who is giving it. I cannot transfix you with war stories about dodging bullets and defying generals, because I have never covered a war. I cannot dazzle you with inside dope about the White House, because I have never been inside it except as a tourist. I have written investigative series on poverty, political corruption, and Medicaid fraud, but I cannot present myself as a career muckraker like Wayne Barrett or Lowell Bergman. Whether at article or book length, I have spent much of my career exploring subjects that are not considered the sexiest or the most prestigious—culture, religion, education, immigration. If you give me a choice, I will always prefer to write about someone obscure than someone famous. And, as much as I savor the company of fellow journalists at a party or in a newsroom, I feel like I've done something wrong if I bump into any of them reporting the same story as I am.

In my idiosyncratic way, though, I have had the kind of career that you may have, or at least the kind that is common in our profession. I've moved from a small paper (*Courier-News*) to a medium-sized one (*Suburban Trib*) to a major one (*The New York Times*), and I've gone on to write six books, counting this one. Over the past fifteen years, I have taught journalism at Columbia University as well, and my students have gone on to write books of their own and to report or produce for such news organizations as National Public Radio, *The New York Times*, the *Los Angeles Times*, NBC, *Rolling Stone*, and *BusinessWeek*.

By teaching, in addition to doing, I've been compelled to think about what it takes to be a journalist and what it means to be a journalist. In my classes, and now in these letters to you, I've had to put the precepts into words. When I first took an adjunct-instructor position at Columbia, I did it as an agnostic on the whole notion of whether journalism even can be taught. My undergraduate journalism courses at the University of Wisconsin had been, with one or two exceptions, an utter waste. The college paper, the *Daily Cardinal*, was my classroom, and experience was my teacher. The mentors I met along the way were editors and veteran reporters, not members of any faculty. Still, I told my first Columbia class that it had the power to change my mind, and it did. I came to understand the intense education that can happen in the "conversation" between a student's article and my editing. I was affirmed in my belief that intellectual curiosity and a relentless work ethic matter infinitely more than natural ability in achieving excellence.

I have also seen, over the years, some of what makes journalistic education fail, and that is when it settles for being a bunch of hero-worshipping students fawning over a star writer's war stories. I remember the weakest student in my first Columbia class asking if he could skip a session so that he could hear a speech by David Halberstam. "If you go to hear Halberstam," I told him, "you'll never *be* Halberstam." The real David Halberstam took his first reporting job on a paper in West Point, Mississippi, with a circulation of four thousand. Now in his seventies, he still prides himself on conducting two full-length interviews a day, every day, when he is doing research for a book. As for my long-ago student, who blew off class for the speech, I can't say that I've ever seen his byline.

In a book like this one, of course, I cannot be your line-editor, though I hope that some of what I write may help teach you how better to edit yourself. There are other things, too, this book does not mean to be. It is not meant to be a textbook, or a history, or a work of media criticism, though elements of all those forms may appear from time to time. Nothing in a book, mine or anyone else's, can provide the specific, situational guidance a young journalist receives from a gifted editor. I was fortunate enough to cross the path of several, and I wish you the same luck and opportunity.

What, then, can I do for you? I hope I can teach you the way a journalist encounters the world—as reporter, as writer, as citizen. I hope I can instill you with certain habits of mind and inspire you to develop both a work ethic and a moral ethos. I have spent virtually my entire career in print journalism, but the things I can tell you about craft, integrity, intellectual curiosity, and concern with the human condition are every bit as applicable to someone working in radio, television, or online. And if I speak to you about painting or music or drama, and I'm certain that I will, then I want to introduce you to art that will elevate your cultural literacy and, if I may be so bold, enhance your life. The greatest journalists never settled for only reading or watching or listening to journalism; they looked for their models and catalysts in literature, film, jazz, every great art.

I envision you as the high-school and college journalists I once was, as the graduate students I now teach, as the young reporters I worked alongside on my first jobs. I remember the yearning, the ambition, the impatience, the hunger to improve. I am interested in excellence and I am only interested in teaching those who aspire to excellence. As I sometimes tell my students in moments of exasperation, "I take your work seriously. The question is whether *you* take your work seriously." I promise to pay you the compliment of high standards. I see myself as your elder, not your superior. My credibility comes less from my successes than from my failures. I have erred in every way I will warn you about. As a minister of my acquaintance once told his congregation, "Church isn't a museum of saints. It's a hospital for sinners."

So I welcome your company. I am flattered by your attention. In the end, I want you to believe, as I believe, that you have chosen a profession of consequence and value, a profession that requires no apology, a profession that can make you happy.

Radical Tradition

I had no way of realizing it back then in the summer of 1975, but the newspaper culture I was entering was soon to pass away. Typewriters, glue pots, wire-service tickers, linotype operators, morgues with envelopes of clippings, afternoon newspapers—all must seem as foreign to you, as antediluvian, as *The Front Page* era was to me. As I drove my family back from a Thanksgiving dinner a few years ago, my son was nagging me to buy him some cutting-edge (and obscenely expensive) computer product. When I refused, he hissed, "You're so old, your expiration date has passed." My daughter enjoys tugging on the sagging flesh that has begun to bunch around my elbows. I have gray hair and bifocals. But as I type, I see my hands, lean and sinewy and threaded with veins, as if the very act of writing has kept them in fighting trim, no matter what else in me has aged.

So don't expect me to concern myself much with what is trendy in journalism at this moment in time. I've lived through eight-track tapes, Beta recorders, and laser discs; I've heard how infidelity can keep a marriage lively and cocaine isn't an addictive drug. Trendiness is overrated when it isn't outright wrong. My concern is with tradition. I am the product of two institutions steeped in tradition, *The New York Times* and Columbia Journalism School. I don't mean tradition as a set of rote reflexes, as formulas repeated ad infinitum, as a fig leaf for laziness. I mean tradition the way you hear it in a song by Muddy Waters or Hank Williams, not necessarily something ancient, but something venerable, something tested, something durable and true.

The value system that I have in mind—that a journalist is an honest broker of information, which has been assiduously reported, verified for accuracy, and written without bias or partisanship—is a product only of the past century, as Michael Schudson made clear in his indispensable history *Discovering the News*. American journalism actually began as an overtly politicized, highly opinionated enterprise, a low-tech version of today's blogs and talk shows. It was a radical step for journalists of the early 1900s to actually conceive of their work as a public service, untainted by personal belief, rather than an act of advocacy. It was a radical step for them to believe they could transcend their predispositions and bend their judgments to accommodate what they learned in the act of reporting.

By the time I started out in journalism, these doctrines had gone unquestioned for decades and were ripe for being challenged. My colleagues and I spent our official working hours in newsrooms that subscribed to the ideal of objectivity, then went home to read the magazines that were inventing the passionate, personal, and dissident New Journalism—*Rolling Stone*, the *Village Voice*, *New York* in its Clay Felker heyday. Our efforts felt pallid in comparison; we subscribed to the rules of attribution, interviewed people on both sides of issues, and tried to remember to get their middle initials. Sometimes it seemed that we didn't trust our readers to know anything without our informing them. On the *Suburban Trib*, the copy editors had a convention of inserting definitions of any terms thought to be specialized or obscure. Hitler, lest anyone be unclear, was a "notorious World War II dictator." Islam was a "religion practiced by Muslims."

These days, though, I find the tradition almost revolutionary, if only in contrast to the cynicism and venality all around. As the author (and Columbia dean) Nicholas Lemann has pointed out, opinion journalism occupies an ever larger share of the media landscape. Between blogs, talk-radio, and the intensely niched worlds of the Internet and cable television, nobody need ever encounter a fact or analysis to contradict the beliefs he or she already holds. I've heard of viewers who watched Fox News Channel so unceasingly that the network's logo was eventually burned into their television screens. Instead of the marketplace of ideas, we have ideological echo chambers, Rush Limbaugh for one crowd and Air America for another. The very concept of a journalism that honestly sifts and sorts through a day's events is the subject of ridicule from Left and Right alike. They jointly spout the same pejorative acronym—MSM—for the mainstream media. With its slogan "fair and balanced," Fox has managed to transform the cardinal virtues of our profession into a sneering joke.

My own bitter joke is that I remember when the *New York Post* published nonfiction. By that I mean that I remember it before it was bought by Rupert Murdoch. I'm not generally a believer in the Great Man Theory of History, but in Murdoch's case, his despotic genius has been to infect contemporary American journalism with some of its most pernicious diseases. He transformed the *Post* from a spunky and serious paper to a gossip-and-sensationalism rag, created the tawdry genre of tabloid television with the show *A Current Affair,* and bankrolled Fox News Channel, a political movement masquerading as a news organization. No individual bears more responsibility for degrading the profession I practice and adore, and I would feel no differently if Murdoch had been a demagogue of the Left rather than the Right. There are certainly enough conspiracy theorists and professional scolds from that side of the spectrum.

I'm counting on you to join the battle. I realize you're too young to remember journalism being any other way than it is in its present affliction. Let me give you just one example of how it was, and of how it possibly could be again, at least in your hands. Radio and television stations used to be subject to a federal regulation known as the "fairness doctrine." It basically said that in exchange for free use of the public airwaves, the government required them to make a good-faith effort at political balance in their programming. The stations also were required to commit some portion of their broadcast day to public-service programming. Some of the results were pedantic; a few, I have to admit, were downright laughable. When I was out promoting my first two books, I often wound up taping public-affairs shows for rock-and-roll stations, which would broadcast them in some black hole like six on Sunday morning.

Still, whatever its flaws, the fairness doctrine and a whole journalistic sensibility it typified was far superior to what has replaced it. Since the doctrine was repealed by the Federal Communications Commission in 1987, and as the public-service requirement has gone largely unenforced amid a climate of deregulation, a sizable part of commercial radio has turned into Republican Party mobilization and indoctrination, with no pretense of alternative voices except for the token liberal cohost who functions as the resident punching bag. (And I have little doubt that many Democrats wish they could figure out the same formula.)

There is something daring, then, in believing, as I believe, that journalism must do more than pander to prejudices. There is something daring in letting your own attitudes and orthodoxies rub up against inconvenient realities. There is something daring in taking on a burden of expertise, proving by your own example that being a journalist means more than putting up a Web site and saying you are.

We'll talk more about these issues later on, I'm sure, but for now I just want to suggest to you that the tradition is worth mastering. I don't mean that every journalist should work only in the mainstream. In my own career, after all, I've written dozens of opinion essays and infused my books with a subjectivity that would have been anathema to the news columns of a daily paper. But I do mean that the tradition is the irreplaceable foundation; the tradition is the place to start. I think there's more to learn by looking out the window than by looking in the mirror, more to learn by listening to others than by talking to yourself. As one of my former colleagues at Columbia, a famously curmudgeonly editor with a bullwhip on his office wall and the appropriate name of Dick Blood, used to tell his students, "It's called reporting. You ought to try it sometime."

The Shape We're In

I wish I could tell you that you're entering a world that welcomes, respects, even reveres you. I wish I could tell you journalists are regarded as heroes, the way they were when I started college in 1973. Bob Woodward and Carl Bernstein, Tom Wolfe, Seymour Hersh—they made reporting look not only courageous but cool. In my dorm, my friends and I battled to be the first to get to read each fresh edition of *New Times*, a magazine that broke the Karen Silkwood story, among many others. I didn't know a single classmate who was majoring in business.

The other morning, just before I began writing to you, I was flipping through the *Times* when I came to the headline "Survey on News Media Finds Wide Displeasure." The article reported the latest in a series of despairing studies of public attitudes toward the media. This one, conducted by the Pew Research Center for the People and the Press, found that the bitter red-state/blue-state divide on political issues was carrying over into views of journalism as well. More than 40 percent of Republicans in the Pew survey said news organizations were hurting democracy, while 54 percent of Democrats said the media were too soft on President Bush.

These findings came only months after an even direr report, *Trends 2005*, also based on Pew polling. It found that nearly half the respondents said they "believe little or nothing" in their daily newspaper—a position held by only 16 percent in 1985. Public confidence in the press, which registered at about 85 percent in 1973, has slumped below 60 percent for the past decade. A majority of respondents think the press can't even get the facts straight and is politically biased, besides.

Having entered journalism during the Nixon era, when many journalists landed on the official White House enemies' list, I am accustomed to an adversarial relationship between government and media. It's nothing new, either, for administrations to try to shape news in their favor. Before anyone had ever applied the word "spin" to media manipulation, Franklin D. Roosevelt was accused of it. John F. Kennedy interceded with journalist friends to kill impending articles on the Bay of Pigs invasion. Never before the Bush administration, however, have I experienced efforts by the government to actively subvert journalism itself—by paying off pseudo-journalists like Armstrong Williams to promote Bush policies in his syndicated column; by credentialing an impostor named Jeff Gannon with the White House press corps so he could lob softball questions during presidential news conferences; by inserting overseers in the public-television system and trying to do the same with public radio. A federal grand jury's investigation into leaks about the CIA led to the jailing of a *New York Times* reporter, Judith Miller, for refusing to identify anonymous sources, and, even more disturbingly, the capitulation of *Time* magazine to the demand that its reporter Matt Cooper testify before the jury.

Ultimately, Miller did testify with the consent of her source, vice-presidential aide Lewis Libby. Now that Libby has been indicted on perjury and other charges, his trial could very well include the spectacle of reporters taking the stand in the prosecution of a government source, a complete abrogation of their promise of confidentiality. These events add up to something different than the normal, healthy tension, the clash of legitimate interests, between Washington and the Fourth Estate. Long after anyone but trivia buffs can remember the names of the players, the climate of suspicion will be making your job all the more challenging.

We journalists, let's face it, have supplied plenty of reason for such pessimism. The shape we're in is at least partly a result of the state we're in. Dan Rather retired in disgrace from CBS after one of his *60 Minutes* episodes— on George W. Bush's spotty record in the National Guard during the Vietnam War—was found to be based on a forged document. *Newsweek* retracted a report that American interrogators at the Guantanamo Bay prison camp had flushed a copy of the Koran down a toilet to humiliate Muslim internees. That error, seized upon by the Bush administration, undermined much accurate reporting on abuses by U.S. interrogators. The past few years alone have seen high-profile plagiarism and fabrication cases such as those involving Jayson Blair and Michael Finkel of *The New York Times*, Jack Kelley of *USA Today*, Ruth Shalit and Stephen Glass of the *New Republic*, Mike Barnicle and Patricia Williams of the *Boston Globe*, and David Brock of the *American Spectator*.

While the news organizations involved have plunged into soul-searching about what went wrong, the perpetrators themselves have made transgression a terrific career move. When Janet Cooke of the *Washington Post* had her Pulitzer Prize revoked twenty-five years ago because she had invented the award-winning story of an eight-year-old heroin addict, she at least had the good grace to vanish from public view, winding up as a saleswoman in a shopping mall. Many of the next generation of plagiarizers and fabricators got six-figure book contracts. Glass was the subject of a feature film. Brock became a darling of the Left by disavowing his own right-wing attacks on Anita Hill and Bill Clinton. Personally, I can see a valid case for just cutting off their hands.

The public has its own role, though, in this pattern of degradation. From the widespread criticism of the media in those Pew surveys, you'd think that viewers and readers were just craving first-rate journalism, longing for it. You might want to read an article by Michael Winerip from *The New York Times Magazine* entitled "Looking for an 11 O'Clock Fix," or rent a documentary film by David Van Taylor, *Local News*. From Orlando (in Winerip's case) and Charlotte (in Van Taylor's), they tell the same essential story. One television station in a very competitive market decides to abandon the popular emphasis on crime—"If it bleeds, it leads," as the TV-news aphorism goes—and give the public the kind of serious, nuanced, issue-oriented program the public always claims to want. In both cities, the experiment drives the audience away.

We live in a time when expertise is denigrated, when professionalism is considered suspect. Hardly anyone remembers that the term "bureaucrat" entered our lexicon as a compliment, indicating a civil servant who had been hired on the basis of merit rather than political connections. In writing a weekly column on education for the *Times* for the past several years, I have noticed that one of the leading qualifications to be a big-city school principal or superintendent is the absence of any classroom experience. So it doesn't surprise me, and it shouldn't surprise you, that a trained, practiced, professional media is pilloried as a distant, arrogant elite. When we are distant and arrogant, we surely deserve the barbs. When we are excellent at our work, qualitatively superior to the amateur or hobbyist, then our excellence requires no apology.

I'm not trying to scare you off. I hope you find the challenges inspiring. When I was your age, the cachet of journalism attracted plenty of poseurs. One thing you can say about the present unpopularity of journalism is that it drives out all the uncommitted. If you're a true believer, if this is meant to be your life's work, then nothing and nobody can change your mind. Even in a bleak period for journalism, you can find signs of vitality—the astounding growth of NPR; the development of *Salon* and *Slate* on the Internet; the transformation of *USA Today* from an object of ridicule to a serious, successful national paper; the opening of twenty-four-hour cable news operations in local as well as metropolitan markets.

So don't think journalism is going away. Delivery systems may change from paper to computer, and reporters may be renamed "content providers." Revered and beloved publications may perish while reality-TV series thrive. But intellectual curiosity, vigorous research, acute analysis, and elegant prose will never go out of style. If anything, the shorter the supply, the more those traits will be valued.

Several years ago, while writing a book about American Jewry, I came upon a famous essay reproaching Jews for their perpetual fear of extinction; it was wryly titled "The Ever-Dying People." During my years as a *Times* reporter, I covered Broadway, which for decades thought itself so close to demise that it was nicknamed "The Fabulous Invalid." One of the hit shows while I was on the beat, "A Chorus Line," has a piquant moment you might appreciate. A dancer named Bebe has just been cast for a show, and naturally enough she feels like celebrating. Yet all around her the rest of the chorus members are complaining—"no security in dancing," "no promotion and advancement," "no work anymore." To which Bebe shoots back, "I don't wanna hear about how Broadway's dying. Because I just got here."

■ Temperament

In Egyptian mythology, there existed a god named Thoth. He was usually portrayed with a body of a man and the head of an ibis, and often he held a palette and a reed stylus, the accoutrements of a scribe. In the underworld, Thoth questioned the souls of the dead to determine the quality of their earthly lives. As each person's heart was weighed against a feather to measure its purity, Thoth recorded the result, which meant nothing less than the soul's fate for eternity.

The Egyptians considered Thoth the god of writing, magic, time, and the moon. I think of him as the deity of journalism. I keep a small statue of Thoth in my office, and I frequently show it to my students on the first day of class. Some of journalism's many critics would find a bitter irony in my veneration of Thoth. To them, one of the worst things about journalists is the way they play God—a judgmental, unfeeling, omnipotent God, inflicting pain for sport, wielding power without account.

I find a different symbolism in Thoth. To me, and I hope to you, as well, he represents the moral mission of journalism and journalists. Thoth observes and interviews and analyzes and evaluates, all the things journalists do, and he must act with integrity and accuracy, because he does indeed command destiny. If he fails, the very cosmos cannot function. And if we fail, democracy suffers the wound.

I am not afraid to speak of journalism as a moral calling—as a vocation, in the priestly sense of the word—because I am not afraid to hold myself to a moral standard. I am not afraid to sound naïve or sentimental. There is an old saying that anyone who's not a socialist at twenty has no heart and anyone who's not a capitalist at forty has no brain. Along the same lines, anyone who doesn't enter journalism believing it is a moral enterprise might as well move straight on to speculating in foreign currency or manufacturing Agent Orange. There will be disappointments enough over the course of your career; your initial idealism must be a pilot light, flickering at times, but never extinguished.

I was recently reading one of the seminal texts about journalism, *Liberty and the News* by Walter Lippmann. Writing eighty-five years ago, long before Noam Chomsky or the Iraq War, Lippmann was decrying the press for "manufacturing consent," specifically for the American entry into World War I, by elevating patriotism above truth. He was bemoaning a corps of reporters who had little education, scant expertise, and no particular desire to acquire either. So Lippmann was no Pollyanna, no Pangloss. Yet he was capable of this ringing call, this righteous sermon:

> The news of the day as it reaches the newspaper office is an incredible medley of fact, propaganda, rumor, suspicion, clues, hopes, and fears, and the task of selecting and ordering that news is one of the truly sacred and priestly offices in a democracy. For the newspaper is in all literalness the bible of democracy, the book out of which a people determines its conduct. It is the only serious book most people read. It is the only book they read every day.

In the twenty-first century, of course, fewer and fewer daily newspapers are published and fewer and fewer Americans read them. Nothing, however, has changed the role that Lippmann espoused for journalism. If anything, in the clutter and clamor of a digitized, globalized world, in the confusion between fact and opinion, in the blurring of information and entertainment, and in the shift from edification to advocacy, we journalists have never been more essential.

Being moral is not the same as being moralistic. I do not urge you to carp and sniff at human frailty from the sideline. I do urge you to bear witness. I urge you to celebrate moments of human achievement and unearth evidence of human venality. I urge you to tell the story. I urge you to be accountable, to your public and to yourself, for what you do and how you do it. As I write to you today, a sunny morning in July 2005, terrorists have bombed the subways and a bus in London. Perhaps it takes such a tragedy to remind all the cynics that however we choose to access the words, sounds, and images—on the *Guardian* Web site, on CNN, on NPR, or in the low-tech newsprint of the *Times*—we desperately need the professionalism of professionals in order to make sense of the world. The bloggers and cell-phone photographers in London can provide the raw material, verbal and visual, but they cannot synthesize and distill it into journalism's "first draft of history."

To be witness, observer, and storyteller, and to develop and refine the skills of each, is to accept the burden of independent thought. It is to reject the easy comforts of conventional wisdom or popular dogma. It is to welcome the dissonance of human events and render that dissonance with coherence and style. All of these exercises stretch the brain and all of them elevate the spirit. As journalists, we eschew such language and resist such definitions for ourselves. We want to feel like populists. So, interestingly, one of the most profound descriptions of the journalistic temperament comes not from a practitioner but from a legal scholar turned university president, Lee Bollinger of Columbia University, who was writing here not of journalists at all but rather of professors:

> I would say the most valued [trait] is that of having the imaginative range and the mental courage to explore the full complexity of the subject. To set aside one's preexisting beliefs, to

hold simultaneously in one's mind multiple angles of seeing things, to allow yourself to believe another point of view as you consider it . . . The stress is on seeing the difficulty of things, on being prepared to live closer than we are inclined to the harsh reality . . . [and] of being willing to undermine even our common sense for the possibility of seeing something hidden. To be sure, that kind of extreme openness of intellect is exceedingly difficult to master, and, in a profound sense, we never do. Because it runs counter to many of our natural impulses, it requires both daily exercise and a community of people dedicated to keeping it alive.

When you find that kind of journalism, much less produce it yourself, your pulse can't help but quicken. You know all over again, and yet with the revelatory force of the first time, what journalism can achieve. Over the years, I've seen that glorious complexity in Thomas Edsall's political coverage in the *Washington Post*, with its insistence on hearing and taking seriously the experiences of individual voters. It's the quality that makes J. Anthony Lukas's *Common Ground* the totemic book of narrative nonfiction for me, as it lends equal weight and dignity to the disparate, often contradictory experiences of three families during Boston's school-desegregation crisis. Recently, reading so much reportage from Iraq, I have felt that the dispatches of George Packer of *The New Yorker* have risen above almost all others because they manage to hold in tense dialectic two competing truths—that Saddam Hussein was a murderous despot who deserved to be overthrown, and that the American occupation has been an undermanned, disorganized calamity. (Packer's reportage on Iraq also is available in the book *The Assassins' Gate*.)

There is not only integrity but drama in the clashing visions and versions of reality. You can especially appreciate that in two works of oral history adapted for the theater, David Hare's *Via Dolorosa* and Anna Deveare Smith's *Twilight: Los Angeles, 1992*. In each case, the playwright turned journalist to interview a deliberately wide range of participants in a deeply controversial episode—for Hare, the conflict between Israelis and Palestinians; for Smith, the riots in Los Angeles after the acquittal of the white police officers who beat an unarmed black man, Rodney King—and then enacted the edited transcripts alone on a bare stage. The effect of such theater, as in much memorable journalism, is to force the audience to reconcile, or at least appreciate, opposites, to acknowledge the knotty, gnarled shape of life.

What I am espousing here is something much deeper and more probing than the formulaic on-the-one-hand-and-on-the-other-hand type of news report. To open your journalistic mind to divergent, even diametrically opposed perceptions of the world is not to surrender to relativism. Why was it, for instance, that blacks and whites evaluated the same evidence in the O.J. Simpson murder trial so differently? It does not make Simpson any less guilty (in my view) to sort out why the defense's narrative of a black man framed by bigoted white cops rang so true for African Americans.

Indeed, if that circus of a trial had any larger meaning, anything to remotely merit the volume of coverage it received, it was as an arena for the "reverse reality" of white and black Americans.

Let's take this point a step further. To plumb the experiences and motivations of terrorists is not to exculpate them. The author James Baldwin understood that distinction when he once observed that the ultimate novel about racism in America would be written from the viewpoint of the lynch mob. Several times in my own career, I have written at length about men who committed acts of political violence—a Catholic extremist who bombed several abortion clinics in New York, a Jewish militant who tried to assassinate former Israeli prime minister Shimon Peres for his role in the Oslo accords. My purpose was not to condemn acts that were plainly heinous; my purpose was to provide a reader with an understanding of what drove these men, who were also capable of acts of great tenderness, to aspire to murder. The journalism we require in our bloody present will make sense of the jihadist strain of Islam, not to excuse it, but to comprehend it.

Fairness can be a false refuge as well as a cardinal virtue. Not long ago, the cable network C-SPAN decided it would broadcast a speech by the Holocaust historian Deborah Lipstadt only if it were followed by a segment on David Irving, the Holocaust denier who had brought and lost a libel case against her. The implication here was that the Holocaust wasn't a fact, merely a contention open to debate. When Charles Murray wrote his book *The Bell Curve*, which purported to prove that blacks were genetically less intelligent than whites, few journalists made the effort to examine whether his scientific evidence was plausible. Instead, they treated the subject of racial inferiority as one easily dealt with through he-said/she-said impartiality. Most recently, in covering the campaign against evolutionary biology by adherents of "intelligent design," too many journalists have presented the two positions as equally valid, worthy of on-the-one-hand, on-the-other-hand symmetry. In fact, for all but a handful of scientists, evolution remains the accepted explanation and "intelligent design" a pseudonym for biblical creation.

Part of your challenge will be to learn and master what you don't know rather than to hide behind your ignorance. Being versatile is different from being facile, and being called a "quick study" is being damned with faint praise. It takes time to acquire expertise. It takes time to hear out the innermost truths of individuals. It takes patience and wisdom to even think about playing God.

The Journalist as Human Being

To be a moral journalist, you must retain your humanity. You might think I'm stating the obvious. Yet the ideal of objectivity calls for journalists to be detached from those whom they cover; dispassion is seen as the guarantee of fairness. Personally, I have always thought "objectivity" was the wrong word, anyway, because human beings cannot help but be subjective. What we strive for as journalists is better thought of as fairness, and that topic itself is worth a separate discussion a bit

later. Whether you call it objectivity or fairness or anything else, journalistic distance cannot and should not
always override the rest of our nature. Journalism is
about channeling emotions, not turning them off. And
on some rare and extraordinary occasions it is about
tearing down the barrier—what theater people call the
"fourth wall"—separating us from the people and events
we are reporting. If you can't be a person, then you'll
ultimately be less of a journalist.

The story of two prize-winning photographs and the
men who took them goes right to my point. If you've
studied the Vietnam War, you've probably come across a
photograph of a Vietnamese girl running naked and
howling down a road, the victim of a napalm attack by
U.S. troops. That single searing image played no small
part in deepening opposition in the United States to the
war, and it also won the Pulitzer Prize for the photojour-
nalist Nick Ut of Associated Press. What very few people
knew was that after Ut finished photographing the girl,
Phan Thi Kim Phuc, he brought her onto a minibus, ordered it to a hospital, and pleaded with doctors to attend
her right away. Only after Kim Phuc was on the operating table did Ut head to the AP bureau to deliver his film.
Twenty-eight years later, in a ceremony before the
Queen of England, Kim Phuc said of Ut, "He saved my
life." I would add that he also saved his own soul.

The other photo came out of the Sudanese famine in
1993. It caught an emaciated toddler at the moment she
collapsed while struggling to reach a feeding station; in
the background perched a vulture. Like Nick Ut, Kevin
Carter, the freelancer who took the photo, helped to

galvanize public opinion with the image. As much as any other single factor, it led President Bill Clinton to deploy the U.S. military on a humanitarian mission in the region. Again like Nick Ut, Carter was honored with the Pulitzer Prize. Unlike Ut, though, he did not intercede to save the subject of his photo. One of Carter's frequent comrades, David Beresford of the British newspaper the *Guardian*, recalled asking him, "What did you do with the baby?" Carter replied, "Nothing, there were thousands of them." (At other times, Carter did say he chased away the vulture and that he cried for hours after taking the photo.) Less than four months after winning the Pulitzer, Carter committed suicide. You can never know the exact thinking of anyone who kills himself or herself, but in the aftermath many of Carter's former colleagues kept thinking about the day he let the journalist in him crowd out the human being.

I know how difficult it is for someone like you, new to the profession and trying to acquire the proper temperament, to parse these dueling claims on your conscience. I know because I was teaching an introductory reporting class at Columbia Journalism School in September 2001. My students were barely a month into their journalistic education on the morning Al Qaeda attacked. Still struggling to learn the most rudimentary techniques, they were instantly hurled into the biggest story since World War II. Unlike some of my faculty colleagues, I didn't send my students down to Ground Zero, fearing for their safety, but I did assign them to report on the aftermath of the attack as part of covering their neighborhood beats around the city. I can say, in retrospect, that the experience made them transcend themselves. They wrote about Dominican-immigrant janitors killed when the Twin Towers collapsed, Sikhs subjected to bias crimes because they were mistaken for Arabs, undertakers preparing stray body parts for burial, the Fire Department bagpipers' band that played hundreds of funerals and memorial services and lost two of its own men.

In the process of reporting those stories, my students also collided with some anguishing and necessary questions. What if someone I'm interviewing cries? Can I touch them? Can I hug them? What if I cry? Am I a bad journalist if I do? My adjunct instructor in the class, Mirta Ojito of *The New York Times*, stepped in to answer. For weeks after the attack, Mirta had been writing for "Portraits in Grief," the *Times* collection of profiles of every identified victim of the Al Qaeda attack. In other words, she was spending virtually every working day interviewing survivors. She told the class about how she had cried over the phone as she spoke with the father of two daughters killed in the Twin Towers. She recalled going into the women's bathroom at the *Times* and finding a colleague there sobbing from the strain. Mirta understood that the tears didn't undermine her as a journalist. To have been unable to feel, and thus to convey, the heartache of those widows and widowers, those parentless children and childless parents—that inhuman remoteness would have been a journalistic failure.

One of the students Mirta and I taught that fall was Kerry Sheridan. The articles Kerry did back then about the Fire Department's band led her over the succeeding year to write an exceptional book about the group, *Bagpipe Brothers*. More than most journalists of any age, Kerry was plunged into the ambiguous borderland between journalist and person and was forced to determine both an ethical code and the terms of engagement. She wanted to write a great book and she also wanted to be able to sleep at night. I asked her recently what she would tell you. "In times of tragedy, lines get blurred and the best advice I could give a young journalist on keeping your humanity is to allow yourself to bend with the breeze," she said. "Observe, be content to be in the background, help if you can, but don't make that your priority. Think of how you would feel if your family was in that situation. And carry tissues."

Loyalty Oaths

I want to warn you about loyalty oaths. I'm not referring to the formal sort of allegiances government employees were forced to sign during the McCarthy era, the kind that destroyed lives and careers by leaving the taint of Communist subversion on anyone principled enough to refuse. I'm thinking here of the implied, unspoken loyalty oaths typical of our own era, with its passion for ethnic, racial, or religious roots and its fervor for identity politics. The more you feel part of a community, or the more a given community claims you as its own, the more pressure will be directed at you to serve that community's perceived interests. You will be expected to hush up "bad news," however that happens to be construed, or to advance whatever is the ideological agenda du jour.

Years ago, when I was just starting out as a *Times* reporter, I happened to be invited to a Passover seder. Hearing my surname and *New York Times*, one of the other guests launched into a diatribe about how I was "a self-hating Jew, the worst kind," and, for good measure, how the *Times* was anti-Israel and anti-Semitic. After a baffled, buffeted moment, I realized my antagonist had confused me with Thomas L. Friedman. Personally, I couldn't have imagined higher praise. At that time, Friedman was on his way to winning his first Pulitzer Prize for his coverage of the Israeli invasion of Lebanon, while I was covering disputes about predawn garbage pickup in swanky Connecticut suburbs; the closest I got to my renowned namesake was mistakenly receiving his issues of *College Hockey* magazine in the office mail. None of this placated the seder critic. Even if I wasn't that Friedman, I was a Freedman, a member of the tribe, and my Jewish identity was expected to trump all others.

I can certainly understand the frustrations of people who feel as if they're pressed up against the glass of a journalistic enterprise that grinds away oblivious to their presence. Latinos, lesbians, evangelical Christians, whatever group you can think of—it sees one of its own on the inside, with access to all those magical levers and switches, and naturally enough wants that person to pull them on behalf of the group. Journalists themselves are not immune to the temptation. I've known a number of black reporters and editors who felt deeply torn between wanting to cover black issues, because they believed they could do it in a more sensitive and nuanced way than whites, and desperately wanting not to be typecast as being only capable of covering their own people. The reporter on a political campaign for months at a time, the reporter embedded with a military unit, the reporter spending an entire season with the same sports team— they, too, become subject to the presumption of loyalty.

At bottom, however, a journalist must always be a free agent, responsible to the craft, the value system, and the readers. (Or listeners or viewers.) Group loyalties, or even mere affinities, must never become your internal censor. Your friendships and family bonds may be strained or even broken as a result. The candidate, the colonel, the quarterback all might call you a backstabber. As relentlessly social as journalism can be, in this respect you're going to have to prepare yourself for a certain kind of loneliness.

Several of my journalistic colleagues have put this ethos in particularly eloquent terms, and you might draw strength from their examples. One of my finest editors and mentors was Jeff Schmalz. He was only a few years older than me, but he'd started on the *Times* as a copyboy while an undergrad at Columbia, and by his late twenties he oversaw most of metropolitan coverage. Of the gays in the *Times* newsroom then, in the relatively homophobic climate of the early 1980s, Jeff was one of the handful willing to be open about his sexuality. While fiercely devoted to the *Times* as an institution, he never stinted on criticizing its coverage, or lack thereof, of gay issues. I think he saw in some of his young reporters on the Metro staff a chance to bring about a change. My

first year on the paper, he sent me to cover the Gay
Pride Parade, where I bumped into a high-school classmate, whom I inadvertently outed by quoting him in my
article. Jeff assigned a heterosexual Marine veteran,
Mike Norman, to a major series on New York's gay community, even tipping off Mike about which clubs and
bathhouses he ought to explore.

So when Jeff himself left the editing desk to turn reporter, and when he later took on the AIDS beat, you
might have expected him to play the role model, the ex-
emplar, the credit to his race. Rather, he measured his
professionalism in distance. Then, in late 1990, the space
between reporter and assignment grew narrower. Jeff
crumpled to a heap in the newsroom, and an examination
for the cause of the seizure revealed he was suffering
from full-blown AIDS. He had so few T-cells left, he
should have been dead already. Jeff recovered for a time,
and he returned to the beat. He was more compassionate
now, less smug, with those he interviewed, more willing
to share embraces and tears. Still, he came under excruciating pressures from gay-advocacy groups, as he recounted in a memorable essay, which was published a
year before he died in 1993 at the age of thirty-nine:

"Who are you?" a TV reporter asked me at a
funeral march in Greenwich Village for an Act-
Up leader dead of AIDS. The reporter knew full
well who I was: the guy from The Times with
AIDS.

The lid of the coffin had been removed, the
open box carried on shoulders in the rain, led in

the dusk by mourners with torches, the dirge of a single drumbeat setting the pace of this, a funeral turned protest against President Bush's handling of AIDS.

"Are you here as a reporter or as a gay man with AIDS?" the TV correspondent persisted, shoving a microphone in my face. His camera spotlight went on.

I didn't respond. People in the crowd moved closer; they wanted to know the answer. I wanted to know it, too. Finally, it came out: "Reporter." Some shook their heads in disgust, all but shouting "Uncle Tom!" They wanted an advocate, not a reporter. So there I stood, a gay man with AIDS out of place at an AIDS funeral, an outsider in my own world.

I walked back to the office in the rain, thinking along the 30 blocks about how tough it must be for blacks to report about blacks, for women to report about women. Yet that kind of reporting is the cutting edge of journalism. Some people think it is the journalism that suffers, that objectivity is abandoned. But they are wrong. If the reporters have any integrity at all, it is they who suffer, caught between two allegiances. . . .

I didn't write an article about the funeral march, judging it worth only a picture and a caption. I passed the journalism test that afternoon in the rain by failing the activism test. To turn activist would mean that AIDS, not reporting, would define me.

In one respect, Jeff had it lucky. As a *Times* reporter, he enjoyed the protection of a vast, powerful institution, one that was imperious and impervious in the face of external pressure, at least until the Jayson Blair scandal. Not every journalist will reach such a lofty station, and very few journalists of your age will start out there. I certainly didn't. If you are like most of us, it will be when you are on the staff of a smaller or more specialized news organization, the kind that is more vulnerable than the *Times* to public outcry and even economic boycotts, that you'll find out what kind of backbone you have. Which brings to mind an editor named Gary Rosenblatt.

I first encountered Gary as a competitor. In 1987, the *Times* put me on the story of the first Jew ever to be charged with war crimes against Jews. His name was Jacob Tannenbaum, he lived in Brooklyn and belonged to a synagogue there, and he was alleged to have beaten and whipped Jewish inmates in the forced-labor camp at Gorlitz, Germany. I confess that I did a thin, dismal job on the story, settling for the portrait of a beloved neighborhood fixture, clearly implying he'd been falsely accused. Speaking of group loyalties, in retrospect I think that as a Jew I could not admit the reality of Jewish collaboration with the Nazis. Shortly after my piece appeared, a Jewish weekly from Baltimore published an account of its own. The reporter did what I had failed to do. He traced inconsistencies in Tannenbaum's statements over the years, and he tracked down survivors of Gorlitz, who provided firsthand descriptions of Tannenbaum raping women, torturing men, and enjoying favored treatment from the Nazis. (Indeed, the following year, Tannenbaum pleaded guilty and was stripped of his citizenship.) I had to admit I'd been scooped, completely out-reported, and I was curious who had shamed me. The reporter was Arthur Magida, and his editor was Gary Rosenblatt.

Six or seven years later, Gary moved north to take over as editor and publisher of the *New York Jewish Week*, the sort of paper that traditionally played the role of communal cheerleader, heralding sundry Jewish achievements and omitting any evidence to the contrary. Clearly, Gary was not going to be that kind of booster. Yet, at the same time, he was deeply enmeshed in the community he had promised to unflinchingly cover. He lived in a heavily Jewish suburb, Teaneck, New Jersey, and belonged to a synagogue there. His children attended Orthodox day schools, yeshivas, and colleges. Even more immediately than Jeff Schmalz, he was going to hear every complaint, feel every pressure. And if you start your career on a local daily, as I did, or on a local TV or radio station, then you will know the experience only too well. You will be living among your audience, running into it at the Laundromat, the bar, the bakery.

In June 2000, Gary wrote a front-page story about allegations that a prominent Orthodox rabbi had physically or sexually abused teenaged boys and girls over a thirty-year period. This was not an investigation built on the rickety stilts of anonymous sources. Scrupulously, Gary required every victim he quoted to speak by name, on the record. He delineated these people's efforts to have the offending rabbi, Baruch Lanner, disciplined within the Orthodox establishment, efforts that repeatedly led to Lanner being protected and allowed to continue his educational and pastoral work with young people. Gary even took the extraordinary step, prior to publication, of seeking counsel from an Orthodox rabbi who is an authority on religious ethics about whether to publish these highly explosive findings. He told Gary it was a judgment call.

After the article appeared, the outcry resounded. One rabbi delivered a sermon calling on the *Jewish Week* to fire Gary. Two others, without being so specific, accused him of breaking Judaism's taboo against *lashan hara*, spreading malicious gossip. Hundreds of e-mails and letters poured in to Gary, evenly divided between hailing and reviling him. He had smeared all rabbis; he had washed dirty linen in public; he was embarrassing Jews in front of gentiles. "I told them our job is to describe the community as it is, not just as we'd like it to be," Gary said. "Sometimes, people don't want to look in the mirror."

Perhaps the ultimate confirmation of his decision came a year and a half later, when a scandal about pedophiliac priests erupted in the Catholic Church. Although vaster in scale than the Lanner case, the Catholic situation contained many of the familiar elements—clergy whose abusive pattern was well-known to superiors; a religious hierarchy that quashed or ignored credible complaints from children and parents; and attacks on investigating journalists for being sensationalistic or antireligious. Gary made contact with one such writer, Rod Dreher of the *National Review*, and pointed up the parallels. Dreher wrote back, "I don't know if you're observant or not, but I am a devoutly observant Catholic, and I see exposing this kind of horror as a religious duty. I've had a couple of very high-level priests, including an archbishop, tell me I really should back down, as a 'good Catholic.' I told them they misunderstood me: that I write about this not in spite of being Catholic, but because of it."

When Gary printed Dreher's words in a column in the *Jewish Week*, he added his own punctuation. And I will echo it here: Amen.

Do We Betray?

I tell you these stories to fortify you. You're going to hear plenty to the contrary, so be prepared. You're going to hear from professors steeped in deconstructionist theory that there is no such thing as a fact, no such thing as truth, no such thing as history, only narratives created by oppressors to control the oppressed. You're going to hear all about the failings of journalism from bloggers and media critics who've never left their computers long enough to cover a fire or a city council meeting. You're going to hear from readers, listeners, and viewers who lash out at the messenger bearing a disquieting message. Sometimes those people will be right. Your only defense is the quality of the work you do. You must be willing, and indeed eager, to defend every iota of it.

Sooner or later, you are bound to encounter one very specific criticism, one that strikes right at the heart of journalism's moral purpose. It comes in the form of a book by Janet Malcolm, *The Journalist and the Murderer,* which is widely read among journalists and widely taught in journalism schools. In her opening sentences, Malcolm writes: "Every journalist who is not too stupid or too full of himself to notice what is going on knows that what he does is morally indefensible. He is a kind of confidence man, preying on people's vanity, ignorance, or loneliness, gaining their trust and betraying them without remorse."

Malcolm's indictment pierced the journalistic community. And it did so, paradoxically, because it spoke to a quality she clearly believes journalists lack: a conscience. A journalist, indeed, does seek to put people at ease, to win their trust, by suspending, or appearing to suspend, judgment of their opinions. During an interview, a reporter will listen more attentively and patiently to what a subject has to say than will almost anyone else in that subject's life—boss, spouse, neighbor, relative. Many people will confuse an open ear with a promise of friendship, and some journalists, to their discredit, will encourage the misapprehension. The relationship between journalist and source, with each seeking some advantage from the other, is filled with ambiguity. You can see that process of mutual manipulation indelibly portrayed in the relationship between Mel Gibson as an Australian reporter and Linda Hunt as his fixer in revolutionary Indonesia in Peter Weir's film *The Year of Living Dangerously* (based on the novel by Christopher J. Koch). Precisely because so many journalists do consider the consequences of their actions, they felt convicted by Malcolm's critique.

There is a big difference, however, between self-scrutiny and self-disgust. Before you take Malcolm's thesis too much to heart, you ought to know a few things about it and her. Malcolm erected her broadside against all journalists and all journalism by focusing on one especially flawed practitioner, Joe McGinniss. Malcolm's book mercilessly reveals how McGinniss insinuated himself into the confidence of a Green Beret officer accused of murder, Jeffrey MacDonald. While professing to believe in MacDonald's innocence in order to gain access to the jailed suspect and his defense attorneys, McGinniss had actually come to conclude the man was guilty. He went on with the ruse long enough to collect the material for what would become a best-selling book, *Fatal Vision*. The mere fact that MacDonald, by then convicted of murder, sued McGinniss for libel should tell you how extreme McGinniss's ethical failure was. As if to underscore the point, McGinniss went on to write a book about Senator Edward Kennedy that turned out to contain fabricated scenes. So Joe McGinniss no more represents the community of journalists than Jeffrey MacDonald does the community of military officers.

The journalist whom McGinniss may most closely resemble is Janet Malcolm herself. Malcolm had her own *Fatal Vision* episode in writing a *New Yorker* profile of the psychoanalyst Jeffrey Masson, the director of the Freud Archives in London. The lengthy article depicted Masson as an arrogant braggart and included scores of direct quotes in which he essentially hung himself. Insisting that Malcolm had invented several of those utterances, Masson sued for libel. And, very interestingly, a number of the quotations at issue turned up nowhere in

Malcolm's tape-recorded interviews. In 1993, a federal jury found for Masson, determining that Malcolm had fabricated five quotes, two of them libelous. On appeal a year later, Malcolm narrowly won a reversal, even though the jury agreed she had invented two quotes. Another year passed and then—well, gee whiz!—Malcolm's granddaughter knocked some books off a shelf in the writer's vacation home and what should tumble out but a notebook with all the missing quotes. You can decide for yourself just how credible that story sounds.

Janet Malcolm is neither the first sinner nor the last to diminish her sin by saying everybody does it. Every journalist probably does, at some point or another, leave behind a source who feels aggrieved, undressed, abandoned. But admitting there are flaws in the system is far different from saying that every journalistic encounter inevitably, inexorably leads to betrayal.

Whenever I bump up against Malcolm's thesis, I think of one of the magazine writers I most admire, Mike Sager. I've been reading Mike's work for at least fifteen years, since stumbling onto a fascinating article in *Rolling Stone* about a bunch of Vietnam veterans who had washed up in Thailand after the war and never come back to the United States. I didn't realize that piece was Mike's first in a major magazine after having built his craft as a city-desk reporter on the *Washington Post*. Over the years with *Rolling Stone*, *GQ*, and *Esquire*, Mike has made a specialty out of profiling extreme behavior—crack gangs, white-collar heroin addicts, pornographers, swingers, pit-bull fighters, the self-proclaimed Pope of Pot. Mike himself can cut a pretty extreme figure; he generally wears all black and he was the first white person I knew to shave his head. Yet his career has also been a study in ethics. His genius as a journalist has always been to locate the stunningly ordinary and prosaic qualities of the seemingly deviant, to close the psychic distance between Them and Us. To accomplish this, Mike routinely spends weeks inhabiting the lives of his subjects, gaining their trust and intimacy, and then, of course, telling the world what he has found. And he has not, as Janet Malcolm would posit, run a shady game of bait-and-switch. Mike put it this way to me recently:

> When someone agrees to be interviewed, it is our job to explore that person's value system without prejudice. I call it suspending disbelief. If you can't put aside your preconceived notions, you can't find the shades of gray that make journalism and life most powerful. We must sit and listen. Sympathize and empathize. Try to understand.
>
> Then you go home. You turn the volume back up on the disbelief filter. If the person's lying, it will be clear. Chances are, by listening, by letting the person talk, by seeking to understand, you learned a whole lot more. And then, when you sit down to write, the deeper understanding leads to a deeper telling of the truth.
>
> Once, I was assigned to write a long feature piece about a man who weighed nearly seven hundred pounds. We spent weeks together. We

hung out, went places, albeit slowly. I acted as his friend. Over time, I came to care for him as a person. Sensing this, he opened up to me even more.

When it came time to write the story, I pulled no punches. I mean, this guy was so fat, he couldn't properly clean himself when he went to the toilet. He had to have special spraying equipment attached to his commode. I wrote about this, of course. It's fascinating. But the reason I learned about it is only because I had become close to Charlie in a human way. And when I wrote about it, being close to Charlie in a human way, I did so with dignity.

When he read the story about himself, something like 7,000 words of intimate detail, he said over the phone, in a little boy voice, "I feel naked." Looking at this detailed telling of his piece was like standing before a mirror, something he *never* did.

But then, he posted the piece on his own website. He sent it to all his friends. The story was a big hit. Thin people were amazed at the excruciating detail. And fat people were amazed by the dignity of the telling. It was all there but it wasn't mean.

And Charlie and I are still in touch.

There is a point to this story, a point larger than de-bunking Janet Malcolm, and it goes back to Thoth. All journalists play the role of Thoth, weighing the heart and recording the fate. A moral journalist, a journalist in full possession of both professional ethics and human empathy, the kind of journalist I pray you want to be, prepares for the day when he or she must stand before Thoth to be judged.

■ Reporting

Nearly twenty-five years ago, during a vacation from my reporting job on the *Suburban Trib*, I picked up a novel by the Argentine author Manuel Puig. *Kiss of the Spider Woman* takes place in an Argentine prison during the Peronist dictatorship's "dirty war" against dissidents. The plot consists almost entirely of a series of conversations between two cellmates. Molina, a gay window-dresser, has been convicted of "corruption of minors," and Valentin, a Marxist rebel, of instigating strikes at two auto plants. The authorities have placed these two together, we learn much later in the book, with the goal of enticing Molina to inform on Valentin in exchange for lenient treatment and early release.

For day after tedious day, Molina passes the time by recounting in minute detail the plots of his favorite movies. They are romances and thrillers, mostly, mere fluff, and even as Valentin listens for diversion's sake he can't help but disparage them. "I don't believe in that business of living for the moment," he says at one point. "There's no way I can live for the moment, because my life is dedicated to political struggle." Valentin is right about Molina's naïveté. One of the movies he describes in rapturous tones follows the love affair of a Nazi officer and a Parisian chanteuse in occupied France. The villain is a Jew in the resistance. Carried away by the plot, Molina does not even realize that the movie celebrates the same kind of fascism that governs Argentina and has jailed him. Yet Valentin needs the escapism more than he dares to admit. He screams out with nightmares about the torture he has endured and the names he gave up under torment.

Gradually, each man learns something vital from the other. When prison guards give poisoned food to Valentin in a plot to weaken him for interrogation, Molina cleans and nurses him, showing a humanity that requires no ideology. In their cell several nights later, the men make love. Instead of betraying Valentin, Molina agrees that after being released, he will make contact on the rebel's behalf with the underground. He is shot dead by government agents in that act of friendship and idealism. Valentin, burned and beaten by prison guards in retaliation, endures the agony with dreams of B-movies, the kind Molina used to spin out in their cell.

Kiss of the Spider Woman has stayed with me over the years, unlike many other novels. Partly, of course, its longevity attests to Puig's literary brilliance. But I have also clung to the book for what it says about being a journalist. Just as Puig sees Valentin and Molina as the complementary parts of a human being—pleasure and purpose, creativity and idealism—I see them as the complementary parts of a journalist. Valentin knows there must be a story worth telling, and Molina knows it must be told well. Valentin knows issues matter, and Molina knows narrative matters. Molina without Valentin is empty entertainment; Valentin without Molina is tendentious dogma.

Let me put it in even more accessible terms for you. Valentin is reporting and Molina is writing. Valentin is the part of every journalist that wants to be a social reformer, and Molina is the part that longs to be an artist. They are interdependent, inextricably bound, raveled together. You must master both to excel at our profession. But you must approach them in a certain deliberate sequence.

Showing Up

Reporting enables writing. And reporting begins with the decision to report. Woody Allen once observed, "Eighty percent of success is showing up," and Nicholas Lemann has said, "It often seems to me that at any given moment ninety-nine percent of the journalists are covering one percent of what's happening in the world." Far from being flip, those aphorisms get at an immensely meaningful point. There is no reporting without the energy, intellectual curiosity, independent spirit, and sense of social mission required to get out the door and into the hurly-burly.

Pete Hamill has called journalism "God's profession" because "no other work so consistently reminds its practitioners of the persistence of human folly, and mankind's amazing capacity for evil and virtue, stupidity and the endless weakness of men." Whether covering Congress or the town board, the Yankees or Little League, Hollywood or the high-school musical, we are seeking to fathom the same essential forces. Chemistry teaches us that every entity in the world—the keyboard on which I type, the chair in which I sit, the lamp that illuminates my desk—can be reduced finally to the components listed on the Periodic Table of the Elements, the iron or hydrogen or sodium. As journalists, I believe, we explore what might be called the Periodic Table of Human Nature. Every life, whether celebrated or obscure, contains the same fundamental emotions, love or hate, ambition or indolence, exhilaration or despair. We just need to drill down deeply enough to discover them.

For me, no part of reporting has been as fascinating or as demanding as this quest. Like you, I'm sure, I was trained to believe only what is observable and quantifiable. One of my favorite aphorisms advises, "If your mother says she loves you, check it out." Journalists feel most secure with the batting average, the stock price, the body count, the vote tally (well, maybe not in Florida in 2000). We feel comfortable watching the Rose Bowl game or the ticker-tape parade unfold before our eyes. And I don't diminish the effort involved, because it takes exercise to sharpen our senses and use them all. I'll have more to say about that soon enough.

Some of the highest drama, though, takes place behind the eyes and between the ears. It involves what literature calls "interior life." I can remember the moment I realized that this realm was territory for journalists as well as novelists or dramatists. It was a

Sunday morning in the early 1980s, and I had just bought the Sunday *Times*, a hard-to-find treat in the Chicago suburbs back then. On the front page of the Arts & Leisure section was an article about the current Broadway hit, an homage to Duke Ellington called *Sophisticated Ladies*. Being both a theater lover and a jazz fan, I dove right in. What I found was something unexpected, something revelatory. Rather than dealing with the show itself, the article centered on the man who conducted the orchestra, Ellington's son Mercer. The author seemed to have entered Mercer Ellington's very psyche, laying bare the tormented relationship he had had with his father, who was at once inspiration, absentee, and ruthless competitor.

I had never read anything quite like it. I took note of the byline, Michiko Kakutani. If it is possible to get a crush on someone just from their writing, I did. Over the succeeding months, covering my education beat in the suburbs, I spun this fantasy for myself of getting hired by the *Times* and marrying Michiko Kakutani. Well, half of it came true. And when I reached the *Times*, I had the luck—no, much more than luck, the life-changing kismet—to come to the attention of Arthur Gelb, who had been the mentor to Michiko, Frank Rich, and Maureen Dowd, among many others. I spoke to Arthur about the Ellington article, and how it had staggered me. "A great reporter," he told me, "has to be a great psychologist."

More than a decade later, when I was new to the Columbia faculty, a student gave me an essay that expounded brilliantly on Arthur's insight. It had been written by Thomas Gavin, a novelist who had also done several years of newspaper reporting just out of college. Clearly, he had thought a lot about what the writers of each genre could learn from the other. "My slender knowledge of what a journalist does," he wrote, "reinforces my deeper knowledge of writing novels to suggest that the truth of *fact* a journalist must honor above all is closely related to the truth of *motive* that is a novelist's primary allegiance. There is a juncture, I believe, where the passions of the journalist and the novelist meet."

At a very practical level, what Arthur Gelb and Thomas Gavin meant was that an interview is not a regimented Q&A or an adversarial interrogation. At least, it should be an interrogation only when the subject matter demands such an approach. That felt right to me. I have never been the inquisitor sort. I have always disdained the ambush style of *60 Minutes* and the hyperbolic combat of political talk shows; they provide the worst models possible for people like you. Arthur and Gavin told me, and now I tell you, that it is permissible, even desirable, to converse rather than fire away, to use human intuition in framing questions, to demonstrate empathy. To this day, one of the two questions I ask most often is, "And how did that make you feel?" (The other is, "And then what happened?" David Halberstam has said his favorite is, "Who else should I be talking to?")

Skillful interviewers, by nature, function alone, in the field. You cannot observe one at work like a medical student watching a master surgeon in the operating theater. The closest thing to a tutorial I can recommend is the public-radio show "Fresh Air." I think of Terry Gross, the host, as a print-style interviewer, because she does not seek bombshell disclosure or the raucous confrontation, those sound-bite staples of entertainment, but rather the increments of experience and reflection. She persists gently. She comes prepared. She does not settle for adjectives and generalities. She laughs when a response amuses her, revealing something of herself.

Tom Wolfe once likened journalists to "beggars with cups in their hands waiting for little droplets." What he was lampooning, I think, was not the journalistic enterprise in general but our tendency to expect revelation and full candor from sources on demand, which usually means during a single, relatively brief interview. You simply cannot expect to earn such trust in a passing encounter, and personally, I tend to disbelieve the subject who has too polished a line of patter waiting for me. My initial interview with a subject usually has more the quality of a topographical survey, an exploratory surgery, and only in the aftermath, reviewing my notes, do I determine where my questions really should focus. The pressure of reporting on a daily deadline cannot be an excuse for the failure to follow up. Cell phones and e-mail have made our subjects more readily available than ever before.

You can rely too much, though, on the spoken word. A large part of reporting, particularly for a profile, involves observing. When you watch a person doing whatever he does, you inevitably capture him revealing himself. I do not mean in the sense of unveiling some terrible secret; I mean simply expressing character through action.

Gay Talese's portrait of Frank Sinatra for *Esquire* magazine in 1966, "Frank Sinatra Has a Cold," is considered one of the most exquisite works of narrative non-fiction. It succeeds despite the fact that Sinatra never granted Talese a promised interview. Many lesser writers would have dropped the story there, or made their futile pursuit of Sinatra the theme of the article. Talese showed up and kept showing up. He watched and listened as Sinatra recorded in a studio, caroused in Las Vegas, chatted with his daughter, acted in a film. By the sheer accretion of detail, Talese created a fully shaded portrait of a most complex man—Sinatra as lout, artist, doting parent, tribal chieftain.

You don't need to be a star writer with a star subject to employ these powers of observation. Richard Marosi of the *Los Angeles Times* was one of my students at Columbia in the mid-1990s, when he was just making the transition from being an actuary to a reporter. For his master's project, which is essentially a magazine article or book chapter, Richard explored the phenomenon of Dominican immigrants in New York supporting their families back home, and by extension the Dominican economy itself, with remittances from their paychecks at relatively menial jobs here. To put the larger issue in human form, Richard focused on a man named Marino Guzman. Over several months of reporting, Richard grew increasingly anxious. Guzman made two hundred dollars a week stocking shelves in a bodega, lived in a windowless room in a Bronx basement, and sent most of his money to a wife and children whom he hadn't seen for seven years. Yet nothing Richard asked Guzman could entice him to speak about his feelings. Richard wondered how could he possibly write seven or eight thousand words about a man who was taciturn, inarticulate, or both? I urged Richard to just stick by Guzman and take plenty of notes, and so he did. Once a month, Guzman permitted himself a single treat. He went to a diner to drink a few beers and listen to a band play the sentimental Dominican music called *bachata*. As Richard sat with him there one night, Guzman began to weep—with exhaustion, with loneliness, with yearning. That scene explained more of Guzman's interior life, his sacrifice, than any soliloquy.

When you report, report with all of your senses. Dick Blood, the former Columbia colleague I mentioned earlier, used to send his students to check on soup kitchens around the city, and when they filed their stories he would invariably castigate them for one reason above all. They'd written all about the poverty, the charity, the scruffy clothes, the matted hair, the wailing babies, but not the soup. "You've got to eat the meal!" Blood would rail. (Taking that advice literally, one of Blood's protégés, Craig Laban, went on to become an award-winning restaurant critic for the *Philadelphia Inquirer.*) When I was working on my book *Upon This Rock*, I needed at one point to research the history of East New York, a Brooklyn neighborhood that had changed rapidly from Jewish to black. I went walking its streets with a middle-aged Jew who had grown up there, and for some reason I asked him, "What did it smell like?" He thought for a moment, then began to rhapsodize about the aroma of corned beef wafting out of tenement windows.

Paradoxically, nobody embodies this ideal of reporting with all the senses better than a journalist who almost never leaves the office. Robert McFadden, a legendary rewrite man on *The New York Times* metropolitan desk, dictates questions to the on-scene legmen who feed him raw material. It is said that a blind person will often develop a preternatural sense of hearing to compensate, or vice versa, and McFadden, there at his computer terminal with his headset, seems to have heightened his descriptive powers in reaction to his chosen quarantine from the outside world. The questions he volleys at his legmen seek not only documentary facts but aura, texture, and emotion. He rarely makes much use of the television monitors in the *Times* newsroom, even though local stations often are covering the same story he is. "What we do," he told me once, "is so much more literate than pictures on TV. You can see a picture of a pile of rubble but what does a pile of rubble look like? That's all in the details and the words. In some strange way, the words are closer than the pictures to the actuality." To put it another way, the picture that counts with McFadden is the one he assembles in his mind's eye from the myriad of questions he asks. On a nearly daily basis, he can transform what might have been a dutiful hard-news story into a tableau.

Let's look—and *look* is the operative word for writing that is this visual—at excerpts from two deadline articles on vastly different topics, part of the package of stories for which McFadden won the 1996 Pulitzer Prize in the Spot News category.

Heavily armed police officers and agents of the
American Society for the Prevention of Cruelty
to Animals crashed into an old movie theater in
the Bronx late Saturday night, seized 296 people
and scores of caged and bloody roosters and shut
down what had been billed as a national
championship cockfight. . . .

It provided a window on a largely secret world
in which birds are crossbred for aggressiveness,
raised on steroids, fitted with razor-sharp spurs,
injected with PCP, or angel dust, to deaden pain,
and set in a ring to slash one another to death
while spectators bet thousands on their favorites
and roar for blood. . . .

The raid at 1000 Morris Avenue, near East
165th Street in Morrisania, also offered a rare
glimpse into a cockfight venue: a converted
theater, nearly the size of a football field, where a
fighting pit and bleachers in-the-round had been
built, along with a labyrinth of false walls
designed to be pulled together in case of a raid to
make it seem as if a boxing match was under way.
A phony boxing ring was even installed. . . .

It slanted down from the lowering sky like
showers of silver javelins. It lashed dusty
windowpanes, beat tattoos on parched leaves and
darkened the bone-dry earth. It dripped from
eaves and ran in silken rivulets into arid gardens
and iridescent streets. The gray windy air was
fresh again with a sense of life renewed.

After months of deepening drought in New York, New Jersey and Connecticut, a soaking, drenching, cooling rain fell for 12 hours yesterday—1 to 2 inches in most areas—bringing nourishment to wilting vegetation, a trickle of hope for sunken reservoirs and welcome relief from a monotonous skein of sunbaked days.

Like approaching autumn, the rain was hardly big news. But there had been less than a quarter of an inch of it in the region since Aug. 1 and yesterday's steady rain, while no deluge, loosened the hardscrabble landscape, left clumps of trees gleaming like emeralds, lightened the mood for rainy-day stay-at-homes and made some who ventured out feel like singing in the rain.

Even the most vivid snapshot, however, remains just that. Reporting requires context, a knowledge of how a momentary event fits into the larger flow of politics or culture or history. The author Russell Banks wrote a stunning novel in the 1980s that wove together the stories of two seemingly unconnected characters bound for Florida. One was a Haitian woman fleeing the Duvalier dictatorship in a wave of "boat people," the other a plumber from a depleted New England mill town looking for a new economic start. Very deliberately, Banks invoked the theory of plate tectonics in titling the book *Continental Drift*. His point, I think, is that individuals often believe they are acting only as individuals, when in fact their decisions and destinies also reflect vast forces of which they are barely aware.

There's a rich lesson for journalists, an admonition, in Banks's thesis.

I like to describe the interplay this way. Imagine two framed pictures, each one a portrait of the same person. In one, the image nearly fills the frame, and in the other it takes up only a small patch of space. These represent two kinds of reporting. The large image stands for everything you can learn from and about the main subject of your article or broadcast. It stands for the most complete interviewing and observation possible. Yet that is not enough. The small image reminds you of all the other research required to put an individual's experiences into context, to relate the microcosm to the macrocosm. Only when you have reported from the image out to the frame and from the frame into the image are you ready to synthesize the two pictures into one, the way our stereoscopic vision lets our brains form a single picture from the separate images on the retinas of two eyes.

If that sounds a bit cryptic, let me put it in concrete terms for you. My book *The Inheritance* describes the ideological realignment in American politics in the twentieth century—from the creation of the New Deal majority to the ascent of Reagan Republicans—through the experiences of three working-class families. At one stage, I was describing a pivotal moment for a young man named Tim Carey. Born into a loyal Democratic family, Tim enlisted in the army during the Vietnam War and as a military policeman was assigned to guard the Pentagon during a major antiwar march in October 1967. The events of that day, when protesters breached the line of MPs and Tim himself was nearly trampled, remade his partisan identity.

I must have spent eight or ten hours interviewing Tim about the experience. I had no reason to doubt his account, because he had proven to be a candid and accurate informant on many other topics. Still, Tim could only be an expert in Tim. To understand more deeply the episode and its meaning, to paint from the frame into the image, I undertook a separate and yet parallel line of research. I located and interviewed three of Tim's comrades from his unit to find out how their memories compared to his. I read the official Department of Defense account of the Pentagon confrontation, as well as the reports in *The New York Times* and the *Washington Post*. I looked through still photographs from those newspapers and film footage from the NBC archives. I read Norman Mailer's *The Armies of the Night*, a memoir of the Pentagon march from a militantly antiwar perspective, and Christian Appy's *Working-Class War*, a scholarly study of how poor and blue-collar Americans like Tim Carey disproportionately served in the military. Only after all that research was I prepared to write the scene, just 4,000 words in a book of 175,000.

In my teaching, I never assign my own books and rarely hand out my own articles. I think I'm still rebelling against college professors who made me ante up twenty or thirty bucks for their tomes. But I often do give my students the passage about Tim Carey and the Pentagon march. It is a teaching tool and a kind of advance obituary for myself. More than with nearly any words I have ever written, I know I can stake my reputation on those four thousand, because I know I did my reporting. I know I showed up.

Scuffed Shoes

I once was permitted to attend a meeting of church elders who were investigating an allegation that a middle-aged male usher had fondled a ten-year-old girl who had skipped out of a Sunday worship service. As the pastor of the church convened the meeting, he said, "I'll check your knees before we make our decision. Anybody whose knees aren't dusty and dirty can't have a say." What he meant, I later came to realize, was that this matter was so grave, he trusted only those who'd been praying for divine guidance. In our field, journalism, I trust only those with scuffed shoes. The nicks in the polish, the ground-down heel, the mud and dust on the instep, all of these attest to the act of reporting. Scuffed shoes are the evidence of enterprise.

There is a whole array of publicists, media consultants, political operatives, sports-information directors, personal managers, and sundry other suck-ups who walk the earth with the sole goal of keeping your shoes spotless. And there is a treacherous group-think within newsrooms and among journalists covering the same beat, a process of reinforcing received wisdom and conventional views of events. When conservatives assail a liberal bias in the media, they are partly (and correctly) identifying a media culture of widely shared assumptions about abortion rights, gun ownership, and religion's role in public life, to name just a few issues.

Over my whole career, I've seen the way these forces, from within and without, try to entice reporters into laziness of both the physical and the intellectual sort. Back on my first full-time job on the *Courier-News*, I worked a Sunday-night shift. Only two or three other reporters were on it, and because of our sparse numbers, the night editor was reluctant to let us leave the office, should any major story break. Yet he also expected us to fill the news columns of Monday's paper. So this very canny mayor of a town I covered would stop by the newsroom on many of those Sunday evenings with a press release extolling his latest achievement—one typical crusade was raising money for a volunteer first-aid squad—and offering himself as an interview subject. The enticement was really no different from what I experienced years later when I covered the theater industry for the *Times* and had press agents by the dozen praising whatever I wrote, bidding for my favor so that I would work up a piece on their client. Most recently, doing a regular column on education, I received hundreds of e-mails a month from public-relations people, and I've become extremely adept with the DELETE function.

Those who are paid to pitch their wares to you, or those who are as plainly self-interested as the mayor, represent the lesser threat to you, because their agendas are so obvious. As I was saying before, you will find it harder to resist the sort of unanimity that can pervade the press corps. You could see this especially acutely during the 2004 presidential primaries, when, almost on cue, the entire narrative switched. *Howard Dean is a longshot. . . . No, Howard Dean, with his Internet fundraising, is the future. . . . No, Howard Dean the crazed screamer is une-lectable and maybe unstable, too.* All these pirouettes oc-curred by the time the first caucus of the primary season had ended, long before all but a tiny fraction of the nec-essary delegates had been won, and the tenor of the re-porting created a self-fulfilling prophecy. I decry this phenomenon not as someone with any special fondness for Dean but as a journalist who looked, often without success, for some journalist with a dissenting point of view, grounded in scuffed shoes rather than the amen corner.

Now, in the digital era, technology itself has proven to be a deeply mixed blessing. I know well enough the utility of databases and search engines, and I use them often myself; some of the best investigative reporting re-lies on sophisticated computer analysis of data. So I am not here to be a Luddite, the journalistic version of the original-instruments movement. But you must under-stand that technology is a tool, not a value, and a double-edged tool at that. Used indiscriminately, technology is just another snare, just another enticement to sloth.

There was history before Nexis, and there is research beyond Google. The very ease of online reporting makes it seductive and dangerous. In both the blogo-sphere and the ever-expanding field of media criticism, I see a version of reporting that eschews human contact and firsthand observation, two things that have an in-convenient way of complicating or contradicting one's preexisting opinions. More treacherously, when you conduct research in cyberspace, you enter a culture that abhors the very concept of editorial oversight. The ethos of open-source sites, like the encyclopedia Wikipedia, is that anyone and everyone can contribute, regardless of expertise or the lack thereof.

"Information wants to be free," goes an Internet catchphrase, but that is not tantamount to saying information wants to be accurate. Several years ago, a student of mine did an exercise, searching both Nexis and the Web for accounts of the Triangle Shirtwaist Company fire. The fire, in a garment sweatshop on the Lower East Side in 1911, is a historical event with an agreed-upon set of facts. Yet the various Web sites and Nexis articles provided different dates, company names, and death tolls. As more journalists do more reporting online, errors echo through story after story, falsity morphing into apparent truth.

This risk is nothing entirely new; it has accompanied every breakthrough in the technology of mass media. The printing press could just as efficiently produce *The Origin of Species* as *The Protocols of the Elders of Zion*. The Internet, though, makes the dissemination of disinformation easier and faster than ever, and harder to discern. One of my Columbia colleagues, Sreenath Sreenivasan, leads workshops on what he calls "smart surfing." When he Googles "Martin Luther King," as an example of naïve research, one of the top sites to come up is run by bigots and devoted to maligning King. It looks so respectable, though, a young reporter might not know the difference.

The most credible reporting is the most original reporting. I mean what you see with your own eyes, what you hear with your own ears, what you acquire with every one of your senses. Beyond all that, I mean *original reporting* in a conceptual way. Whether or not you have a beat, you must approach the world in your own way, deaf to cant, immune to spin, and, perhaps most importantly, unaffected by your colleagues and competitors. Great journalism comes from the curmudgeons, the iconoclasts, the dissidents, the lonely individualists, who insist on pursuing what fascinates or outrages them and tracking it to the ground.

The finest Vietnam War reporters went into the field to compare the optimistic assurances at press briefings to the lived reality of battle. Years before the height of American escalation, David Halberstam and Neil Sheehan found a quagmire in the making; during the peak of the antiwar movement, when U.S. soldiers were routinely reviled, Michael Herr discovered their anguish in besieged Khe Sanh. Perhaps the most famous article written about John F. Kennedy's assassination had nothing to do with the public events. While they were being covered voluminously and redundantly— proving Nicholas Lemann's theorem about 99 percent of the journalists covering 1 percent of the news— Jimmy Breslin of the *New York Herald Tribune* followed his curiosity and instinct in a different direction. What he wrote has lasted:

> Clifton Pollard was pretty sure he was going to be working on Sunday, so when he woke up at 9 a.m., in his three-room apartment on Corcoran Street, he put on khaki overalls before going into the kitchen for breakfast. His wife, Hettie, made

bacon and eggs for him. Pollard was in the middle of eating them when he received the phone call he had been expecting.

It was from Mazo Kawalchik, who is the foreman of the gravediggers at Arlington National Cemetery, which is where Pollard works for a living. "Polly, could you please be here by eleven o'clock this morning?" Kawalchik asked. "I guess you know what it's for."

Pollard did. He hung up the phone, finished breakfast, and left his apartment so he could spend Sunday digging a grave for John Fitzgerald Kennedy.

During the early 1990s, the international media devoted an enormous amount of coverage to the civil war in the former Yugoslavia, and particularly to the attacks by Serbs against Muslims in Bosnia. Perhaps because the conflict was in Europe, perhaps because the faces were white, and perhaps because the victims were Muslims, the issue became almost fashionable in the West. And, certainly, the reports on Serbian atrocities by such journalists as Chuck Sudetic and David Rohde contributed to stirring U.S. intervention, both military and diplomatic, and finally ending the bloodshed. Yet in barely three months of 1994, some eight hundred thousand Tutsis and moderate Hutus were murdered by militant Hutus in Rwanda, and the disparity in media attention is measurable. From 1991 through 1994, the words "Bosnia" and "ethnic cleansing" appeared 12,158 times in news reports, according to the Nexis database. (See, I told you I use it.) "Bosnia" and "genocide" appeared 5,472 times. From Rwanda, there were 2,326 mentions of genocide, and only 347 of ethnic cleansing—despite the fact that the death toll of black Africans was four times greater than that of white Bosnians.

In a grimly appropriate coincidence, Philip Gourevitch, a writer for *The New Yorker,* happened to be waiting in line to visit the Holocaust museum in Washington, D.C., when he saw a newspaper photograph of corpses of massacred Rwandans tumbling over a waterfall. To the degree the American media even covered the genocide, they relied on a standard narrative of ancient tribal hatreds, with the unspoken assumption that there was just nothing to be done about these primitives. None of that made sense to Gourevitch.

"It was a kind of faceless, nameless people that had endured a seemingly indescribable calamity," he later told the *Irish Times.* "It was being described as anarchy or chaos, yet we were being told that 800,000 people had been killed in 100 days. This did not seem either anarchic or chaotic to me. It requires mass organization to create that kind of mass destruction."

Ultimately, Gourevitch made six reporting trips to Rwanda. These yielded several rending articles for *The New Yorker* and then the book *We Wish to Inform You That Tomorrow We Will Be Killed with Our Families.* In tightly controlled prose and unflinching detail, Gourevitch indeed proved that the genocide was not some spasm of disorder or atavistic rivalry but rather an orchestrated campaign undertaken by a totalitarian regime in danger of losing its premium on power. The book was a *j'accuse*, both to the Western nations that stood blithely by and to the media that busied itself elsewhere.

Bethany McLean embodies another kind of independence, freedom from group-think. She was one of scores, if not hundreds, of journalists who wrote about the energy-trading corporation Enron during the late 1990s and early 2000s. Virtually all of them trumpeted the same story: an innovative company with visionary leaders and a soaring stock price. For good measure, Enron essentially bribed several prominent editors and columnists by placing them in advisory capacities, paying $100,000 to William Kristol of the *Weekly Standard* and $50,000 to Paul Krugman of *Slate*. (He later became an op-ed columnist for *The New York Times*.) *Business-Week* listed Enron's executives, Kenneth Lay and Jeffrey Skilling, among the nation's top corporate leaders. *Worth*, *Forbes*, *Red Herring*, and *Business 2.0* all joined the chorus. So did, for that matter, *Fortune* magazine, Bethany McLean's employer.

Amid the hyperbole for Enron, McLean undertook a very basic function for a business journalist. She read through Enron's financial statements. Although she was just thirty-one at the time and relatively new to journalism, McLean had majored in math at college and worked as an investment-bank analyst. She was familiar enough with business numbers to interpret them herself, and in Enron's reports she found signs of financial distress: a rising debt-to-capital ratio, the recent issuance of nearly four billion dollars in debt, sluggish cash flow, a marked decline in profits in one major sector of the company. After she began to ask penetrating questions of Enron executives, they flew to New York, ostensibly to answer in depth, but more likely to pressure her editors into killing the story. Instead, they ran it in March 2001 under the headline, "Is Enron Overpriced?" One emblematic passage stated:

> But for all the attention that's lavished on Enron, the company remains largely impenetrable to outsiders, as even some of its admirers are quick to admit. Start with a pretty straightforward question: How exactly does Enron make its money? Details are hard to come by because Enron keeps many of the specifics confidential for what it terms "competitive reasons." And the numbers that Enron does present are often extremely complicated. Even quantitatively minded Wall Streeters who scrutinize the company for a living think so. "If you figure it out, let me know," laughs credit analyst Todd Shipman at S&P. "Do you have a year?" asks Ralph Pellecchia, Fitch's credit analyst, in response to the same question.
>
> To skeptics, the lack of clarity raises a red flag about Enron's pricey stock. Even owners of the stock aren't uniformly sanguine. "I'm somewhat afraid of it," admits one portfolio manager. And the inability to get behind the numbers combined with ever higher expectations for the company may increase the chance of a nasty surprise. "Enron is an earnings-at-risk story," says Chris Wolfe, the equity market strategist at

J.P. Morgan's private bank, who despite his remark is an Enron fan. "If it doesn't meet earnings, [the stock] could implode."

Less than seven months later, the stock had done more than implode. It had fallen from a high of ninety dollars a share to less than forty cents, and the company had gone bankrupt. Employees and retirees had their pensions wiped out. Enron, it turned out, had been wildly inflating its earnings for years. It had manipulated power supplies in California, forcing statewide blackouts, to drive up prices it could command. Lay and Skilling were to stand trial in early 2006 on charges of fraud and conspiracy. Yet virtually no other reporter had given the slightest indication of trouble in Enron before McLean. For months after her breakthrough article, hardly any competitors followed up on it. Her work is both an inspiration and an indictment. And it indicts journalism just as surely as it indicts Enron.

Tacking

Growing up amid the oil refineries, chemical plants, and landfills of New Jersey, I never had the experience of sailing. My father did own a small outboard, but our weekend outings on Raritan Bay took us to beaches cluttered with empty Clorox bottles and horseshoe-crab shells. We did not dare eat any of the fluke my sister caught. So, only when I was in my mid-twenties and on a trip to Egypt did I learn firsthand what it means to tack. I spent five days plying the Nile on a felucca, the traditional Egyptian craft, and though the boat traveled steadily north, it did not proceed in a straight line. It canted toward the east bank, then angled back to the west, then shifted direction once again, the single sail pivoting on its mast to grasp the wind.

As a reporter, you will be tacking, too, between the shores of truth and justice, trying to hold your direction true north. Our lives would be easier, though much less interesting, if truth and justice were always on the same side, if human events were a pageant of good versus evil. As the Rwanda genocide and the Enron fraud show, there are times when the world does divide in such a polar way, and those times can lift a burden from a journalist's conscience.

What you must resist, though, is the presumption, even the expectation, that issues can be so neatly parsed. If you have gone through college already, then you have probably been imbued with the fashionable theories of our time—deconstructionism, postcolonialism, Orientalism, white studies, and so forth. In varied ways, these theories tell you that all human existence does, in fact, fall cleanly into camps of oppressor and oppressed. The nation, indeed the world, can be neatly divided between whites and "people of color." All virtue resides with the weak; in moral terms, weakness is strength. And any "person of color" is deemed to have the same experiences, values, needs, wishes, as any other, irrespective of differences in nationality, ethnicity, class, and pigment.

These perspectives are not without worth, especially to a young person assembling an adult self. Any sensate human should want to take the side of the underdog.

Guilt is the sign of an active conscience. Undifferentiated compassion is a place to begin. The inherent privileges of white skin, both historical and current, should be recognized rather than merely assumed. As an aphorism of our profession, first uttered by Finley Peter Dunne's fictional Mister Dooley, puts it, "Journalism comforts the afflicted and afflicts the comfortable." If journalists tend to be liberal, and in my experience they do, then the predilection has less to do with ideology than with a more inchoate desire to engage in what Judaism calls *tikkun olam*, healing the world.

None of those values or truisms should overrule the facts on the ground, or, as J. Anthony Lukas called it, "the stubborn particularity of life." Journalism has a weakness for reducing individuals to victims or villains, as if our audiences could not possibly discern gray tones. It sounds admirable to "speak truth to power," as Professor Martin Kramer of Tel Aviv University has pointed out, unless you think of the phrase's implication that you are supposed to tell lies, presumably comforting ones, to the powerless. If you can stay clear of these traps, if you can resist the false reassurance of simplicity, if you can embrace the ambiguity and revel in the nuances, you might come to realize, as I have, that the most compelling journalism rarely takes the form of chronicling the battle between good and evil. In that contest, it takes no great brain or large heart to decide, as the old labor-union song says, which side you're on. The trickier and more valuable task is to illuminate the collision between good and good, or at least between competing versions and visions of what is a good policy, a good community, a good citizen.

When I think about the dialectic between truth and justice, I recall a play by Richard Greenberg, *Eastern Standard*. Greenberg was writing in the late 1980s, when homelessness was a huge issue, especially in his home city of New York. In the play, four yuppies come across a homeless bag lady and in an act of putative compassion invite her to live at their summer house, provided she serve as their maid. To their shock, she winds up stealing from them and disappearing. *Eastern Standard* earned a fair amount of criticism as a result. Weren't people of good will supposed to feel sympathy for the homeless? And weren't the homeless worthy of that sympathy? To me, though, Greenberg had done exactly what a journalist should be doing, poked into all the gray areas. His yuppies were both altruistic and exploitative; his homeless woman was both amusingly cranky and mentally ill. The same instincts that let her survive on the streets also led her to rob her benefactors. Far from making her less affecting, her flaws made her more so, because they made her more fully human.

Let me give you another example, this one from journalism itself. When he was a reporter for the *Wall Street Journal*, Alex Kotlowitz wrote a profile of two brothers and their mother living in the decrepit, crime-ravaged Henry Horner housing project in Chicago. The article created such a stir that Kotlowitz expanded it into a book, *There Are No Children Here*. By many measures, it was an accomplished book indeed. The New York Public Library named it one of the one hundred most important books of the twentieth century. In an era of "compassion fatigue" by many Americans,

Kotlowitz restored inner-city poverty to the political agenda by drastically shifting the angle of vision, focusing closely on children, on innocents.

Where Kotlowitz separated himself from lesser writers on race and poverty was in refusing to settle for easy answers. He saw LaJoe Rivers as both the victim *and* the agent of the misery in which she and her sons, Lafayette and Pharoah, existed. In many ways, in fact, LaJoe embodied the stereotype of the underclass "welfare mother"; at thirty-five, she was the mother of eight children, the first born when she was fourteen, and several of them by this time deeply involved in crime and drugs. Precisely because Kotlowitz portrayed LaJoe and her family so unflinchingly, instead of eliding inconvenient facts, he earned the trust of his readers as a fair broker, a reliable witness. So when he went on to write about how this broken woman spent part of her welfare check on burial insurance for Lafayette and Pharoah, grimly assuming they would die young and violently, he pierced the national conscience.

As someone who has written a great deal about religion, I am struck at how it eludes so many journalists. They try to make it subscribe to their normal framework for understanding the political world—liberal versus conservative, Republican versus Democrat. The Catholic Church in America is routinely seen as a right-wing force because of its opposition to abortion and gay rights; yet that same church has advocated against nuclear arms, welfare reform, and the death penalty, all as part of what the late Joseph Cardinal Bernardin referred to as a "seamless garment" of theology. When we en-

counter evangelical Christians in news reports, they appear invariably as partisans of right-wing causes, which
many certainly do support. Meanwhile, largely unno-
ticed, they have become activists on supposedly liberal
issues such as prison reform, sexual trafficking, modern-
day slavery in the Sudan. But that side of the evangelical
story does not fit our ready template. If you cannot tack,
how will you make sense of a controversy between immigrant Dominican parents who decry the failure of
bilingual education to give their children English flu-
ency and teachers from Puerto Rican backgrounds who
see the Spanish-language curriculum as a civil right?
When I wrote about that conflict in my *Times* column, I
recognized that justice was on the side of the teachers
and truth on the side of the parents. The tug-of-war inside my own brain was the greatest asset I had in telling
the story.

You can go as wrong with pessimism as naïveté,
though, because each is a form of simplistic thought.
Newsrooms are sarcastic, wisecracking places, and their
gimlet-eyed perspective is part of their charm. Journalists as a species remind me of Israelis in one respect. The
greatest insult in Israel is to be called a *freier*, a sucker.
Still, there is a vital difference between being a skeptic
and a cynic, and in the coverage of politics, in particular,
I have seen that distinction increasingly lost. In part, we
can blame the politicians for the pervasive mistrust. It is
the spoor of Vietnam, Watergate, Iran-Contra, the Iraq
War; it is the logical reaction to the "line of the day,"
"staying on-message," and all the other trappings of information management. No journalist I know would

want to return to the complicity between media and government that lulled reporters into avoiding reference of Franklin Roosevelt's handicap and John F. Kennedy's proxy invasion at the Bay of Pigs.

But beware when the pendulum swings too far in the other direction. Beware when you find yourself falling into chic misanthropy, ascribing the basest motives to any public official as your starting point. Being adversarial sounds righteous except when it is a mere reflex, just one more way of imposing black-or-white absolutism on a world washed in grays. I know there are rewards, from the social to the material, for ridiculing politicians, especially those with whom you personally disagree. That sort of attack journalism, all punchlines and adjectives, sells a lot of books these days, fills up a lot of hours on radio and TV. It also has real consequences in degrading the quality of our public life—by reinforcing the nihilistic view that no one's vote much matters and that the two major parties are essentially the same, when both those things have been proven demonstrably false in the past two presidential elections; by ratifying the conventional wisdom that governmental programs don't work and the private sector can do anything better; and by driving quality people out of public service and scaring others from entering. You might want to remember something a former labor secretary, Raymond Donovan, said on the day a jury acquitted him of fraud charges, the culmination of seven years of leaks, innuendo, dubious informants, and massive media coverage. "Which office do I go to," Donovan asked, "to get my reputation back?"

Several years ago, Columbia Journalism School awarded Walter Pincus of the *Washington Post* its annual prize for outstanding coverage of politics and government. The honor came in recognition of a series of articles by Pincus that cast doubt on President Bush's claims about Saddam Hussein's weapons programs. So thoroughly did the articles run against the overall tenor of reporting on the subject, and indeed against the view of both the Clinton and Bush administrations about the Iraqi arsenal, that they did not even make the front page. By the time of the award ceremony in May 2004, Pincus's reporting had been proven prescient.

In receiving the award, Pincus was also invited to address the journalism school's faculty and graduating class. I think most of us expected a speech about perfidy in high places, a rousing call to muckraking. Pincus had spent most of his career, after all, reporting on national security issues, not exactly a vantage point for observing the U.S. government at its most idealistic. Not surprisingly, Pincus spoke incisively and critically about the public-relations apparatus in Washington and the proliferation of photo-ops and other forms of pseudo-news.

But he spoke, too, about his own periods of government service, two stretches of eighteen months apiece during the 1960s as a staff member for the Senate Foreign Relations Committee. He spoke about the importance of staying on a beat long enough to become an expert in it, and about the responsibility of journalism not only to expose wrongdoing but to pursue remedies. Far from describing those he covered as enemies, mere quarry, he reminded all of us that they were "real people, three-dimensional, with spouses and children." Speaking of his own time inside government, he said, "What I saw for the most part were people working hard to solve tricky, complicated problems in ways not visible to the outside world and particularly journalists."

I cannot remember in great detail the audience's response to Pincus. My best recollection is that it was more polite than effusive. The previous year, the columnist Molly Ivins had won the same award, and she had also given a speech. She was a great hit with her well-oiled anti-Bush one-liners. If it was entertainment you wanted, she had it all over Walter Pincus. For wisdom to guide a career, I preferred Pincus, because he comprehended a complex world. He was the one in the rumpled suit and, I'll bet, scuffed shoes.

On Anonymous Sources

Inevitably, a journalist confronts the issue of using anonymous sources. The issue is much on my mind these days because of two recent events. First, a former FBI official named W. Mark Felt revealed that he had been "Deep Throat," the famous informant for Bob Woodward and Carl Bernstein in their Watergate coverage. Then, a federal judge sentenced Judith Miller of the *Times* to prison for refusing to testify to a grand jury about whom she contacted within the government for a prospective article about the outing of a covert intelligence agent.

On the surface, these episodes spoke to the most high-minded view of anonymous sourcing. Were it not for Deep Throat, Woodward and Bernstein might never have been able to expose the Watergate cover-up, and Richard M. Nixon might have finished out his presidency undiscovered. In her act of civil disobedience, Judith Miller was paying a steep price for a vital principle, that a journalist will never violate the trust of a confidential source. Such people often turn to a journalist, a sort of court of last resort, only after having tried the formal channels for seeking redress or reform and being ignored, isolated, or punished. Only the guarantee of protection lets them risk position or career, and the fear of being exposed cannot help but put a chill in the mind of any would-be whistle-blower.

In my own modest experiences of investigative reporting, I have seen the necessity of using and shielding anonymous sources. That first scoop of mine, about the asbestos dump on the canal towpath, came by virtue of a telephone tipster. When I wrote for the *Suburban Trib* about Medicaid fraud and labor-law violations in a chain of nursing homes, and about the unethical way that local highway commissioners ran private paving companies on the side, I received leads and documentary evidence from people afraid to be quoted by name. Just the other week, writing about computer problems in the New York public schools, I depended immensely on employees who forwarded me internal e-mails about the technological fiasco. So, even from my relatively lowly perch, I can fully appreciate why the Woodwards, the Seymour Hershes, the Jonathan Kwitnys, the Wayne Barretts of the journalistic world—those who plumb issues of national and global import—depend so greatly on anonymous sources.

Even as that is true, however, it is an incomplete analysis of the situation. The Deep Throat and Miller cases also offer cautionary tales about the tango between reporter and source. Until Felt declared his identity, the conventional view of Deep Throat was of a heroic and idealistic figure who acted solely in the cause of justice. From what we now know about Felt, it has become clear that he certainly felt those motives, particularly a concern that Nixon was politicizing the FBI, but that he answered to some baser ones, as well. He had been passed over by Nixon to succeed J. Edgar Hoover as FBI director, and in assisting Woodward and Bernstein in their Watergate sleuthing, he was also enjoying vengeance by proxy. It also turns out that Felt's own track record on civil liberties fell a bit short. A few years after helping to topple Nixon, he was convicted of having authorized illegal break-ins of associates of Weather Underground fugitives and had to be pardoned by Ronald Reagan.

The federal investigation that landed Judith Miller in jail, meanwhile, began in response to an investigative story of tainted provenance. It started when a former diplomat, Joseph Wilson, wrote an op-ed essay for *The New York Times* in July 2003 refuting one of President Bush's central bases for invading Iraq—that Saddam Hussein had been trying to obtain uranium from the African nation of Niger. Soon afterward, the syndicated columnist Robert Novak exposed Wilson's wife, Valerie Plame, as a CIA agent. It took no genius to assume that Novak's source or sources fed him that tidbit in order to punish Wilson and terrify any other internal dissenters from going public with their qualms. Here was yet another example of an anonymous source using a journalist to inflict damage. And, unlike in the Watergate scandal, in this case there was no greater good being served. As I write, it remains unclear exactly what role Miller herself played in the deep-background tango between Bush officials and journalists in outing Plame. Those revelations may emerge only when her source, I. Lewis Libby, stands trial.

It did not surprise me to find a welter of motives, some noble and some not, in the Watergate and Plame stories. The sources I dealt with in my own investigative series had all sorts of agendas. Several nurses first alerted me to the Medicaid fraud story and supplied me with a devastating paper trail; my favorite was a bill to Medicaid for providing walking exercise to a patient with no legs. Certainly, those nurses felt a genuine outrage about the abuses, but they also were furious that when the nursing-home chain changed hands, the new, corrupt owner replaced them all with Filipino immigrants. One of my best informants for the stories about unethical highway commissioners was a road worker who'd been fired. Until he got canned, he'd expressed no moral indignation about the way his boss mixed public and private business.

Does this mean I'm advising you against using anonymous sources? No, but it does mean I want you to use them with wisdom, discernment, and discretion. What was it Bill Clinton said about abortion? That it should be safe, legal, and rare. I'd apply the same criteria to unnamed sources.

To this day, I tell my students that if you're trying to decide whom to interview first in an investigative story, figure out who has the most reason to be aggrieved. You go over a Democratic candidate's list of campaign contributors with Republicans, and you do the opposite for the Republican candidate. You let the union rat out the management and the management rat out the union. You identify self-interest and you exploit it.

But that calculation need not be as cynical as it sounds. When you accept information from a source, you are not obligated to accept an entire worldview, a matrix of opinions, emotions, and biases. For that reason, an anonymous source is more useful to you in pointing directions, confirming facts, and, most importantly, providing documentation, than in supplying direct quotation. If you look back over the Woodward and Bernstein articles about Watergate, you'll find that they rarely, if ever, quoted Deep Throat. As they recounted in their book *All the President's Men*, they turned to Deep Throat instead as a sounding board for their suspicions and theories, and as a confirming voice under the *Post's* rule that there be at least two sources for any controversial detail or contention.

That kind of stringency got lost once Woodward and Bernstein became stars, and phrases like "off the record" entered the popular lexicon. In the thirty years since then, journalists have grown far too eager to rely on nameless sources and to let them fire off disparaging or even incriminating quotes from behind the screen of anonymity. I'm not talking exposés of presidential dirty tricks or abusive interrogations at Guantanamo Bay, stories that rise to a stratospheric level of public importance. I'm talking about the garden variety of reporting on government, business, and sports, and, in our gossip-obsessed age, even personality profiles. I've become convinced that, just as animals can smell fear or lust on one another, sources can smell weakness in a reporter, the sort who promiscuously allows anonymity. You have to set a standard for yourself about when to use "off the record" comments that takes account of what a story entails and what a source knows. Is the topic *that* important? Does the source know *that* much? Is there no one else who would know it? Are there no private or public records that would show it?

You will be surprised how often your principled refusal to grant anonymity will force a source to speak by name. Last year, for example, I was reporting a column for the *Times* about a federal law that bars undocumented immigrants from receiving in-state tuition at public universities. I wanted to build the piece around the profile of one student whose future was being imperiled by the law, and so I contacted an immigrant-advocacy organization for help in locating one. From the outset, I told the advocates that I was only willing to interview someone who was willing to be identified by full, actual name—no pseudonym, no initials, no first-name-only. I knew full well that I was, in effect, asking an illegal resident of the United States to put himself or herself at risk of arrest, internment, deportation. I knew these were not idle worries in a period of heightened enforcement under the pretext of homeland security. By holding firm, though, by making it clear that I would not write the column at all if I had to cloak my main character, I eventually persuaded the advocacy group to introduce me to a young woman who was willing to take the risk of exposure in exchange for bringing an important issue, and to my mind an injustice, to light. I'm relieved to say that because of the article, she received scholarship offers from several colleges.

Delighted as I was by that turn of events, what was most significant was the credibility the column gained. In the course of giving speeches about my books, I've often been asked by readers, "Are those the real names?" At the immediate level, the question is literal: Have I given any characters pseudonyms? (Only in a handful of cases, by the way, mostly involving minors.) More deeply, those readers are asking if they can believe my work, if it's factual, if it's truthful. When a rabbi certifies a food product as kosher, it receives an insignia known as a *hechsher*. Actual names are the *hechsher* of a credible work of journalism. And credibility is, finally, all we have.

It's too easy for an anonymous source to levy a dubious allegation from the safe bunker of namelessness, or, in broadcast terms, as a mysteriously backlit silhouette or a digitally scrambled face. The source who speaks on the record may say less, but will say it with greater veracity, because he or she will be accountable. The secret source leaves the journalist alone to answer for inaccuracy, imbalance, even libel. The same Judith Miller who heroically went to prison rather than unmasking a source was herself deceived by anonymous sources several years ago. Those anonymous Bush administration officials and Iraqi defectors told Miller erroneously that Saddam Hussein was acquiring aluminum tubes to use as centrifuges to enrich uranium for nuclear weapons. By the time the article had been discredited, the United States already had invaded Iraq.

In the most flawed hands, anonymous sourcing speeds the path to fabrication. For many years, *USA Today* held to a policy of never using unnamed sources. In deference to the talent of its foreign correspondent Jack Kelley, who was often reporting from war zones, the paper loosened the rule. Ultimately, Kelley was found to have invented quotes and entire persons, and before the scandal was over, he had been fired and *USA Today*'s top editor had resigned. The lesson here is not that all journalists will hide fiction behind anonymous sources; it takes a peculiar personality, about which I'll write later, to want to spend more time and energy concocting a fake story than producing a real one. The lesson is that when all sources must be identified, there is far less latitude for ethical lapses.

Typing and Thinking

When I talk to journalists like you about reporting, one question routinely comes up. *Should I use a notebook or a tape recorder?* So I give my standard answer. I almost always take notes, because something in the physical act of listening that closely and writing that rapidly seems, paradoxically, to open all my senses wider. The one exception comes when I'm conducting an accusatory interview with the subject of an investigative article, because it's very wise for legal reasons to have every question and answer on tape.

But what I want to say is that you've asked the wrong question. These matters of mechanics, like notebook versus tape, make no difference whatsoever to the quality of a journalist. You can etch your notes with a sharp stick onto a clay tablet in cuneiform and succeed extravagantly if you have intelligence and tenacity, empathy for human experience, and appreciation of complexity. Those are the things that matter.

Occasionally, one of my Columbia students will stop into my office while I'm at the keyboard, working on an article or book. They tend to look bewildered at the sight of me pecking out the words with two fingers. How could any professional writer be a two-finger typist? How could you possibly make deadline? I tell them that I'm not a secretary or a stenographer; I'm a journalist and author. There's no reason for me to type faster than I think, because the thinking always has to come first.

◼ Writing

One Christmas season early in our marriage, nearly twenty years ago by now, my wife and I splurged on a vacation in Paris. We made our way one morning to a converted home that had been turned into a museum of Pablo Picasso's work. My fascination with Picasso had begun on the day of the moratorium against the Vietnam War in October 1969, when my favorite high-school English teacher brought in a lithograph of "Guernica," and we spent the class discussing Picasso's famous mural of protest against the fascist bombing of a civilian village during the Spanish Civil War. The young writer in me responded as much to Picasso's style as his politics. The shards and cubes of images, the abstraction of shape, humans with distended features, animals with both eyes on the same side of the head—I assumed that this must have been the way Picasso had always painted.

The Picasso museum, as it happened, was arranged so that a visitor encountered the artist's works in chronological order. With my wife, I literally walked through Picasso's process of development, and what I saw contradicted my uninformed sense of his career. There were line drawings of nudes, pastel portraits, naturalistic studies of the human face and physique. Before exploding the tradition, I realized, Picasso had mastered it.

The epiphany came back to me again last year, when a major exhibit of Romare Bearden's work settled into Manhattan's Whitney Museum as part of a national tour. The show featured the paintings and collages that had made Bearden famous, pieces like "Pittsburgh Memory" and the "Odysseus" series with their fusion of African, American, and Impressionist influences. The line of admirers sometimes stretched out onto Madison Avenue.

At the same time, a far more modest, but in some ways more revealing, collection of Bearden's pieces was hung at the Schomburg Center, sixty blocks uptown in Harlem. This exhibition captured Bearden the craftsman, the craftsman behind the artist. Even at the height of his powers, Bearden put himself through exercises to train his hand to do his eyes' bidding precisely. He drew through carbon paper so he could not see the lines until removing the sheet below, on which the image was reprinted. He did watercolors on graph paper because it absorbed so little paint that it betrayed any excess from the brush. He used felt-tip markers on porous paper so he would not be able to pause without leaving a blemish. All these efforts, all these *etudes*, went toward "getting it in the hand," as Bearden said in a favorite phrase.

I bring up Picasso and Bearden to you because their examples say so much about the process of becoming a writer. What looks like spontaneous creation, divine inspiration, the visitation of the muse, is so much more often the end result of an assiduous work ethic and a conscious effort to develop skills. That should be a liberating message for you. So many of my students over the years have viewed writing as a kind of magic that one either possesses or not. "How do I get a style?" they ask. "How do I get a voice?" I held those same feelings myself for many years. I remember, when I was writing about theater for *The New York Times*, interviewing the playwright David Mamet and peppering him with questions about his creative process. To my exasperation, he kept on comparing himself to a chairmaker, someone who learned to shape wood and fit the pieces together. I left the interview frustrated and indignant, sure Mamet was holding out on his secret. Only years later, maybe that day at the Picasso museum, did it strike me that he'd been imparting a truth I wasn't ready to hear.

You have style and a voice already. They abide in you as parts of your individuality. You would never ask, "How can I learn to talk?" You know that you already have your own favorite words, your own characteristic turns of phrase, your own meter and rhythm. So it is with your writing. When you ask about finding a voice, I'm put in mind of the scene in *The Wizard of Oz* when the Cowardly Lion asks for courage, the Tin Woodsman for a heart, the Scarecrow for a brain, and the wizard tells them they've had those things all along. The medal, the valentine-shaped clock, the diploma he bestows on them provide mere symbols. You can think of your notebook or tape recorder or laptop, if you like, as the same sort of emblems of the writer's style that already throbs inside you.

When you throw off the romantic vision of writing, when you recognize writing is something learned and not bestowed, you are freed and you also are burdened. You lose an elegant excuse for not doing it well, or not doing it at all, the chance to blame everything on that capricious muse. There is nothing supernatural about craft and gumption. To become a mature stylist, as Picasso and Bearden and Mamet knew, is to absorb all the foundational elements of technique—in our case, grammar, usage, and lexicon as well as the specific structures of journalistic prose. It is to clear away all the self-conscious excess or untutored awkwardness that stand between the story you are telling and a reader's or viewer's or listener's ability to receive it. It is to be so much in command of your instrument that you understand why and how you create any given effect. I don't think Picasso painted "Guernica" or Bearden assembled "Pittsburgh Memory" by accident, and I don't think they set out with style more than content in mind. I think they rendered the world the way they saw it, and, with all the acumen and deliberation at their disposal, made the artistic choices they intended to make.

If you'll indulge me one more bit of art history, let me share with you some words from Mai-mai-sze Luch'ai, a Chinese painter of the seventeenth century: "You must first learn to observe the rules faithfully; afterwards modify them according to your intelligence and capacity. The end of all method is to seem to have no method."

The Stages of Writing

What we mean by the word *writing* is a series of actions that begins well before fingers tap keyboard and ends well after the mouse clicks on the SAVE and CLOSE functions. A colleague of mine for many years at Columbia, Carole Agus, described the process in terms of a kind of trinity. "When the reporter in you is finished," she would tell her students, "then the writer in you has to lock the reporter out of the room. And when the writer in you is finished, then the editor in you has to lock the writer out of the room."

Less artfully, I might identify the stages as conceptualization, reporting, outlining, re-reporting, drafting, and revision. By conceptualization, I mean understanding in a deep and specific way the story you intend to tell, being able to boil it down to a sentence, not in order to be simpleminded but in order to be clear. At the same time, you need to stay flexible in your thinking, ready to redefine your topic based on what you discover. Which brings us to the next step, reporting. By reporting, of course, I mean gathering the raw material. At that point, you should take stock of what you've found and try to organize it into an outline. I don't care if you use Roman numerals or circles and arrows, just some way of roughing out the flow of the article. In doing that exercise, you'll very probably find the holes in your research, and so you'll want to undertake a round of re-reporting, more specific and pointillistic than the first sally, which might mean anything from returning to the field to e-mailing follow-up questions. Only when you have all the ingredients you might require are you ready to write a draft. And when that draft is done, you revise it, preferably after having set it aside for a few hours or an overnight, so you can bring a fresh, critical eye.

If I make the process sound obvious, I should apologize. It took me years to recognize and master these steps. Like many young journalists, I embraced the ideal of the single draft. The consummate reporter, I believed, composed straight from memory and notebook. To produce a publishable article in a single pass was the very definition of a pro. I started working nearly twenty years before laptops became common, and so filing a story on deadline from the field meant dictating it over the phone. And I can't say that it hurt me to have learned by trial-and-error how to improvise an article on the spot. My mistake was to ascribe some special value to what would be, in recording-studio jargon, the first take.

A woman named Cissi Falligant was the first person to teach me otherwise. When I started as a reporter on the *Suburban Trib*, Cissi was one of my two immediate editors. With her wispy physique and traces of a Texas accent, she cut an unprepossessing figure in a newsroom with more than a few beer bellies, ethnic jokes, and chain smokers. Then, however, Cissi would start to edit your copy, and you heard the iron will of a woman who had intended to become a literature professor before discovering journalism and who had pursued dance despite congenital lung problems. More than once, I saw a reporter, smarting from one of Cissi's edits, all the more piercing for the calm way she delivered it, stalk around the parking lot outside until the urge to violence subsided.

For me, such a moment arrived when I turned in a profile of a locally renowned special-education teacher. It was my first month on the *Suburban Trib* and I wanted to impress my bosses, so I did twice the reporting I normally would, interviewing children and colleagues and students as well as the teacher herself. I made sure to include a detail or anecdote or quote from every one, just to prove how thorough I'd been. Then I sat at my metal desk in the front row of the newsroom, maybe eight feet from Cissi's station, and waited for my laurel wreath. She summoned me to her side. It was wonderful I had done so much reporting, she said, but what exactly was this story about? What was its point? And how was it organized? Or wasn't it organized? There was a kind of "serpentine quality"— how can I ever forget that phrase?—about it. Cissi told me the piece couldn't be published unless I rewrote it.

Naturally, I thought she was a philistine. In the hundreds of articles I already had written during high school and college, during two summer internships on professional papers, and in fifteen months on the *Courier-News*, I had almost never been asked to make a wholesale revision. In my apartment that night, though, I remembered how my father would sometimes read my *Courier-News* pieces and comment on their wandering style. I had always disregarded the words, since he was not a journalist. Still, he was a machinist, someone with an acute sense of form and function, and now his criticism had been echoed by Cissi, whose journalistic credentials were unassailable.

From that next morning in January 1979 until this one in August 2005, I have never begun to write an article until I knew exactly what it intended to say. I am not suggesting that you make up your mind before you even start reporting; writing gets tendentious fast when a reporter sets out with a made-up mind. But what I started doing at Cissi's behest was identifying the essential theme of an article during the reporting process as a result of what I was discovering. I began to envision reporting as a process of two broad stages. First came the broad sweep, the topographical survey, the exploratory surgery, just to see what was out there. Then came the decision of what one central idea would animate the article, a decision that guided the remaining reporting in a more focused, channeled way. Like building up any neglected muscle, thinking this way felt awkward and unnatural. With a newsroom friend who was also in Cissi's aura, I devised an exercise to help. We called it the "heart-of-the-matter statement." When we were adrift, we would sit down at the typewriter (yes, we were still using them) and write, "The heart of the matter is—." Then, not worrying about making the language elegant, only about making it clear, we would complete the sentence.

Once I knew the heart of the matter, I knew what additional research I needed to conduct. For the first time, I started to outline my articles before starting to write them. With the fervor of the newly converted, I typed out all my notes and put a number next to every fact, quote, or incident that seemed potentially usable. Then I sketched out a kind of flow chart for the article, plugging the numbers into the appropriate places. In the decades since then, I have tinkered with my method, sticking Post-its in my notebooks so that each one becomes a miniature file cabinet, but my essential approach has remained the same. When I recommend outlining to my students, many initially bridle at it, fearing that the time they spend on an outline will push them perilously close to deadline. Speaking from experience, I tell them they will more than recover those minutes, because the outline will save them from winding up in some cul-de-sac.

You need to know that these techniques—identifying a single theme, outlining before writing—are not baby steps for beginners. The most accomplished nonfiction authors utilize them. Robert Caro has won the Pulitzer Prize and National Book Award, among other honors, for his epic biographies of Robert Moses and Lyndon Johnson, each volume hundreds of thousands of words in length. Still, Caro once told a class of mine that he will not commence the writing process until he can express the essence of the book on a single index card. John McPhee of *The New Yorker* occasionally has described his own version of a "heart-of-the-matter statement." When he is struggling to start a magazine article, he begins a letter to his mother, telling her how he's having trouble writing about this-or-that. Having thus explained the story to himself, he erases the opening sentence and continues into the article.

Earlier in this book, I told you about Gay Talese's famous profile of Frank Sinatra, extolling its reporting. A couple of years ago, as part of its fiftieth anniversary, *Esquire* magazine selected the article as the greatest ever to appear in its pages. *Esquire* reprinted the original piece in a glossy chapbook, and, most fascinating to me, it also published a photograph of the several manila folders on which Talese had outlined the article. He laid out six lengthy scenes, each with its date and setting, and he listed the narrative components of each, the scenes, moments, set-pieces. In red ink, to stand out, he noted the emotional qualities he wanted in certain places—"Fear," "Greed," "Things Are Looking Up!"

After studying Talese's outline, I reread the article. It followed the diagram extensively but not slavishly, and that suggests a hugely important point about the relationship between structure and writing. Structure does not constrain writing. Structure liberates writing. When you know what you want to say, when you have made every choice about content based on that firm knowledge, when you have made a thought-through decision about organization, then you can concentrate on the words, the phrases, the sentences.

There used to be a particular panhandler on the New York subway who dressed up like a cartoon Martian and squeaked and squealed away on a soprano sax. "If you give me money," he would tell his captive audience, "I go away." Besides annoying people into paying him, the guy was also capitalizing on a certain view of jazz, especially the so-called "free jazz" of the 1960s, as nothing but random blowing, playing whatever you feel. Don't make that mistake. The greatest jazz musician of that era, John Coltrane, was also the most ardent student of scales. Fellow musicians told stories of dropping off Coltrane at home after a gig and hearing the sound of him practicing again before they had pulled away from the curb. In the liner notes to a boxed set of

Coltrane's recordings for the Atlantic label, the producer and engineer, Tom Dowd, recalled:

> John usually showed up about an hour before the
> session. . . . He would stand in a corner, face the
> wall, play, stop, change reeds, and start again.
> After a while he would settle on the mouthpiece
> and reed that felt most comfortable to him, and
> then he would work on the "runs" that he wanted
> to use during the session. I would watch him play
> the same passage over and over again, changing
> his breathing, his fingering, and experimenting
> with the most minute changes in his phrasing.
> . . . He never lost control: Every step had a
> reason.

All most listeners knew was what they heard on the
resulting albums. The solos that sounded like evanescent
inventions were in fact strung on a latticework of structure. The scales and modes and progressions that
Coltrane had absorbed into his very marrow provided
the foundation for individualism and improvisation. It
should be just so in your prose.

Form and Function

Structure in journalism connotes not only a general
value but a number of specific forms, forms that can
fairly be called traditional. In time, you will need to be
concerned about becoming captive to these forms, repeating them by rote. Early on, though, you will benefit

from trying to master them and from reconciling your style to their demands. I recognize that nothing sounds very poetic in the basic hard-news story or the "human interest" news-feature, and magazine, radio, and broadcast journalism all have their comparable templates. At their best, though, these forms are our sonnets, our haikus, our iambic pentameter, and we gain something by learning how to express ourselves, indeed how to bear witness to the world, within their rigors. When you have accomplished that, and it may take you years, then you will be ready to stretch the tradition, if not step entirely outside it. The Jesuits have a phrase for this: freedom within discipline.

To put it another way, the act of writing is the act of turning chaos into cosmos, of seeking to explain the hurly-burly of existence. Real life takes place in equal increments of sixty seconds to a minute, sixty minutes to an hour, twenty-four hours to a day, none weighted any more or less than any other. A journalist dares to believe that he or she can selectively discern what is most significant from this ceaseless stream of activity and then explain it to the larger society. The basic forms of journalistic prose, if used judiciously, are the tools of doing so. They afford us venerable, proven ways of organizing material, and, more importantly, they compel us to sharpen our thinking.

Something as foundational, as deceptively simple, as a hard-news story demands that we discern what in a given event has the greatest import. The conventional way of organizing hard news was the "inverted pyramid," which posited that every factoid could be rank-ordered in importance and arrayed from most to least; it conveniently served the exigencies of old technologies, in which a printer could toss out the final lines of type from any article that went over the available space. I have never used or taught the inverted pyramid because information cannot simply be rank-ordered. Reporting is more than developing what a lawyer would call a "fact pattern." Within the bounds of fairness and balance, a reporter always analyzes. The sequencing of sentences and paragraphs, the choices of anecdotes and quotations and physical details, all reflect subjective judgment.

The mode I prefer, which I learned from a veteran New York journalist named Lawrence Van Gelder, organizes the opening paragraphs by event, impact, reaction, quote, and scene, each element of which can be expanded and amplified as the article proceeds. A hard-news story also provides a stone against which you whet your voice. It calls for a certain style, a concision and dispassion, a quality my *Times* editor Jeff Schmalz used to call "dead-away." In grasping how to write without inflection, you are implicitly learning how to write with it. Every form you acquire will require you to develop different traits in your writing, like the array of pedals you will see an electric-guitarist use.

There was a time maybe ten or fifteen years ago when hard news was seen as declining in importance, at least in print journalism. Between all-news radio and cable television, a daily newspaper or weekly newsmagazine could never hope to compete. With the advent of the Internet, the very opposite has occurred. Every major news organization now, print or broadcast, publishes on the Web and operates on a perpetual news cycle, in which every tick of the clock is a new deadline. The ability to write hard news—to assimilate information and smoothly render it under withering time pressure—has never been more essential to any journalist entering the profession. Every time a reader loads the home-page of CNN or the *Los Angeles Times* or National Public Radio, he or she expects the twenty-first-century equivalent of the scruffy newsboy hawking a pile of papers just heaved from a bay of a delivery truck, crying out in his ragamuffin slur, "Extra! Get yer Extra!"

Let me show you how Van Gelder's scheme for hard news can work in the hands of an expert. Earlier in the book, I told you about Robert McFadden, the award-winning rewrite man on the *Times*. Here is McFadden doing what he does virtually every day. As you read it, you will see how the paragraphs fill the informational needs, from the event (flood and explosion), to the impact (evacuation, property damage, etc.), to the reaction (repairs already made or under way), to the vivid, evocative quote.

> A century-old water main ruptured under lower Fifth Avenue early yesterday, creating a car-swallowing, curb-to-curb sinkhole and watery chaos in a bustling neighborhood whose streets resembled Venice for a few hours. Then, as the rivers receded, a gas main broke and the crater spewed forth a tower of orange flames.
>
> No one was injured in the spectacular flood-and-fire day centered at Fifth Avenue near

19th Street. But water damaged scores of lobbies, storefronts and basements for blocks around, 40 residents were evacuated, hundreds of offices and businesses were closed, subways were halted, traffic was rerouted and gas, water, electric, steam heat and telephone services were disrupted for many.

By last night, the broken water and gas mains had been capped, the fire had been put out, basements were being pumped out and city officials were gloomily assessing a tangle of damaged water, gas, sewer and electrical lines. Most of the utilities were expected to be restored over the weekend, but officials said Fifth Avenue between 19th and 21st Streets might be closed for a week.

"This one's a beaut," Commissioner Joel A. Miele of the city's Department of Environmental Protection said as he surveyed a gigantic crater that might have been the scene of a bombing or an earthquake. "This one's as good as I have ever seen, or heard of."

Not every news article needs to proceed in exactly this sequence, but every one can benefit from addressing the points in the opening paragraphs. Then, as the article continues, you can return to the event, impact, and reaction in greater depth. Instead of an inverted pyramid, the article resembles a series of ever-larger spirals.

Let's be realistic, though. Any journalist with ambitions as a writer inevitably craves a larger canvas than even the most compelling hard-news story can provide. In time, that might mean a book or the lengthy articles in magazines like *The New Yorker* or *Atlantic Monthly*. More proximately, it means moving into news-features, which might run 1,500 words or so. Like a hard-news story, a news-feature has its own traditional form, which essentially consists of anecdote, context, and exposition. And, like the hard-news form, this one should encourage you to carefully think through your work rather than function on autopilot.

A news-feature is not merely a snapshot, a slice of life. Ideally, it illuminates some larger issue by means of illustrating and embodying it. It links the micro to the macro, the personal or communal experience to the overarching topic. A news-feature must be more than just interesting; it must be enlightening and trenchant. For that reason, you must be careful not to be swayed by the vivid scene, the eloquent quote, the accessible source. Those only matter when they are tethered to something bigger.

In a sense, your reporting only begins after you have reported enough to comprehend your subject. The challenge of writing anecdotally lies in selection and framing as much as in word choice. As in a magazine article or a book chapter, or for that matter a radio or television documentary, a news-feature should unfold with its central character engaged in meaningful action. It should orient the reader to time and place. There is nothing mysterious about withholding information from a reader; there is only needless confusion.

More often than not, I decide upon an opening anecdote only as I am reviewing my notes and preparing to outline. Once I've made the decision, I do the additional reporting, often by phone or e-mail, required to flesh out the anecdote. Again, remember this concept of meaningful action, action that bears on the larger point of the article. I've read far too many leads over the years that described someone sitting back in a chair and taking a pensive drag on a cigarette. That scene only matters if you're writing about lung cancer or tobacco litigation.

If you've begun your article with an appropriate scene, it should lead inexorably into the contextual section of the article. This is commonly called the "nut graf," and I've always loathed the term, because it implies a dumbing-down. Indeed, a cynical aphorism among journalists says that every article has three parts: You tell the reader what you're going to tell him, you tell the reader, and you tell the reader what you just told him. If you can use the form without being enslaved to it, though, then your work will be accessible without being simplistic. Just as your choice of theme guides your choice of anecdote, so, too, will it keep you focused in the expository section of the article. I envision theme as the spine of a gyroscope, around which everything else whirls. If you try to insert a second or third theme, if your focus drifts, then the whole thing topples.

A fierce logic must govern a news-feature, a readiness to discard whatever material does not edify the subject and expand a reader's knowledge of it. Something pretty, something funny, something touching still might belong on the cutting-room floor. Dan Jenkins, the sportswriter and novelist, once said that the definition of being a writer is hearing the best quote you ever heard and knowing when *not* to use it. Or, as William Faulkner said, "Slaughter your beauties."

Keeping in mind our seventeenth-century Chinese artist, the cumulative effect of the hard, deliberate work should be the impression of ease. Only a fellow writer or editor should be able to intuit all the effort; the reader should never realize. Here are the opening paragraphs of a news-feature in the enormously skilled hands of David Gonzales of *The New York Times*, reporting from the village of Bani in the Dominican Republic in November 2001:

> The 15 years that Diego Lugo owned several bodegas in Brooklyn left him scarred with bullet holes in his arm, his leg and his head from three violent robberies. It was the price he paid for a better life, working 12-hour days alongside his wife, Ramona Pimentel, as they saved money to return in 1997 to this town, which they had fled after Hurricane David devastated the island and its economy.
>
> Today, however, the spacious two-story home that they had built selling beer, soda and cigarettes is desolate. The candles they had planned to light Monday night to celebrate their common birthday instead were replaced by a solitary votive light. Mr. Lugo sat sobbing in a wheelchair, trembling at the fact that Ramona, his wife of 36 years, died on American Airlines flight 587, returning home after a brief, but regular, visit with her stateside relatives.

"Fifteen years working in New York for nothing," Mr. Lugo cried, railing at God and his misfortune. "I lost my partner, that is all I accomplished. The greatest thing I had in my life was her. All I want is for God to take me and end this life."

The sorrow inside his house was shared among many residents of this town of about 57,000, 41 miles west of Santo Domingo, where officials estimated at least 15 of their neighbors perished in the crash. The toll reflected both the financial lure of New York City for these scrappy people as well their enduring love for their homeland.

Hopefully, you enjoyed reading those paragraphs. Now think about why. There is nothing extraneous in the opening scene. The language is taut, all nouns and verbs and details, barely an adjective. The narrative moves along efficiently yet without haste, tracing fifteen years of Lugo's life in just five sentences—sacrifice, accomplishment, loss. The prose leads naturally into the quotation, which provides the emotion in the survivor's voice. Then, with a single phrase about how the sorrow was widely shared, Gonzalez connects Lugo's personal experience, the microcosm, to a larger social phenomenon, the macrocosm.

In doing this kind of line-by-line analysis, I don't want to take the visceral pleasure out of reading, to reduce what is ineffable to something merely clinical. But it's worth remembering that the first class every medical student takes is in anatomy, studying a cadaver to learn how to heal the living.

Revering Words, Honoring Language

Seven or eight years ago, I chanced upon a book about a group of monks in the first millennium. This volume bore the grandiose title *How the Irish Saved Civilization*, and it was set in the Dark Ages after the fall of Rome. In benighted, barbarian Europe, the written word and all the knowledge it contained were at risk of dying. Only the monks of newly literate Ireland, toiling with calfskin and quill, salvaged the classical world's wisdom by copying Greek and Roman texts for posterity. Their mission, as the author, Thomas Cahill, put it, "single-handedly refounded European civilization."

I read the book as both history and current events, for in my life as professor, journalist, and author I have felt part of the same struggle against the demise of the written word. In part, I've viewed the enemy as the pervasive visual culture of television, film, and computer graphics, all of which reduce language to the stepchild of image. I've watched with chagrin as schools and colleges fail to teach the basic rules of grammar and usage, leaving me to give graduate students their first lessons ever in misplaced modifiers and noun-pronoun disagreement. Most of all, though, I've had the sense of fighting a battle over aesthetics, of arguing for a certain kind of subtle, dignified, formally correct prose against the slickness that too often passes for literary style, that grab-bag of sentence fragments, clichés, and elaborate metaphors.

Not for nothing did a student once present me with a framed quotation from Mark Twain: "If you catch an adjective, kill it."

For Saint Patrick and the rest of Cahill's monks, preserving literacy must have been a vocation in the Roman Catholic sense of the term, meaning not an occupation but a calling. If you are serious in your aspirations, then you will have to bring to them the same kind of passion. You will have to stand apart from all that is flaccid and lazy in much of the journalism you read, including some that is upheld as exemplary. You will have to resist all the self-conscious flourishes. You will have to respect words. You will have to love and honor language. And I don't mind sounding pedantic or preachy in this cause.

I once dated an actress for a few months, and the experience was a disaster in all respects except one. When I went with her to the theater or the movies, she would always critique the performances afterward. While the audience gave its standing ovations to the most extravagant turns, what my actress admired were the tiny, nearly invisible gestures, the slight lowering of an eyelid, the tensing of a jaw muscle, the incremental shifts in voice. Without realizing it, she was teaching me a lesson about writing.

Or, to be more accurate, she was reiterating a lesson I should have learned years earlier. During the summer of 1977, just after I graduated from college, I had a summer job on the *Minneapolis Star*. I was roiling with literary ambition. I thought of myself as a writer with a capital W. Worst of all, some of my older colleagues on the paper agreed. I had a license for excess. Midway through the summer, I wrote a profile of a parole officer, spending several days with him on his rounds. I became fixated with the image of him as a kind of boatman, guiding his parolees across treacherous waters from the shoreline of prison to the shoreline of straight life. Throughout the article, I worked in all sorts of variations on that theme, and when the piece received a full-page display I felt my artistry had been ratified. Then the editor called me in for a chat. I will never forget what he said. "You think what made the article great was all those water metaphors," he told me, waving an arm dismissively. "What made it great was the quote from that sex offender saying he wanted to run a halfway house for prostitutes."

It took me many years to realize that editor was right. It took enough maturity to come to understand that the role of writing is to serve story, and that there is an essential difference between writing for lines and writing for story. Writing for story requires a trust, in the story and in yourself. Writing for story requires enough confidence not to need to call attention to yourself, not to need to leave fingerprints. Writing for story means modulating your voice so it does not compete with the voices of your characters. It is the insecure writer who feels the need to sound as funny or as dramatic as anyone he quotes. It is the insecure writer who cannot resist underlining the emotions he wants a reader to feel rather than gently, almost invisibly guiding the reader to an epiphany that the reader thinks he came to on his own.

In retrospect, I realize that my adventures in purple prose were a vital part of my growth. Like any prodigal son, I had to wallow in the fleshpots before appreciating the virtues of home. You shouldn't be afraid to indulge all your appetites, too, if only to experience them and get them out of your system. Being abstemious for your whole life would be too much of a bore.

I look back on my own development as a three-stage process. At the outset, infatuated with the mere act of writing, I tried out voices, effects, and wordplay indiscriminately. A few years along, particularly under the influence of Cissi Falligant, I imposed strict limits on myself. Part of this process, which I've already mentioned, involved outlining. For an entire year, I also went on a regimen of holding every sentence in every opening paragraph to twenty-five words or less. I would actually count them. This exercise forced me to value every single word in a way I never had, and to prune away all that was extraneous. As the jazz musician and educator Archie Shepp once told a student who had asked how to play fast, "First you learn to play slow." Finally, having learned to play slow, I emerged into something like journalistic adulthood. I had subsumed the rules so thoroughly that I recognized the specific times when I could break them and the specific purposes this rule-breaking would serve.

Let me give you just one example of the kind of deliberation I mean. In an entire book of a hundred thousand words or more, I may shift from third-person to second-person perspective two or three times, and I will know exactly why I am doing it, what in the material requires the abrupt adoption of an imperative tone. Seven chapters deep into my book *Upon This Rock*, I was describing the tense, distant relationship between a prominent minister and his father. As part of trying to heal that rift, the father drives the adult son to the sugar refinery where he'd worked for nearly forty years, a place the son had never once seen. To viscerally convey the father's sense of having been ignored and unappreciated, I adopted the second-person voice:

> But all his family knew was that Tuesday was payday. They never knew about the desperate men who lined the levee just outside the refinery gate, waiting for you to faint in the heat so they could claim your job. They never knew about the way the raw green sugar clung to your sweaty clothes, attracting roaches and rats. . . . They never knew about how you confronted the union about giving all the crane operator's jobs to white boys and leaving blacks to wield hooks. They never knew it was you, Palmon Youngblood, who broke the color barrier.

When you are ready to lay aside the cheap tricks, when you are ready to write with nouns and verbs, with rigor and deliberation, you will find plenty of instruction, some of it going back to those ancients whom the monks perpetuated. The respect for words begins with tone and vocabulary. In the fourth century BC, Aristotle urged that writing be "clear without being commonplace." Three hundred years later, another Greek (thought to be Longinus) produced a literary thesis entitled "On the Sublime" in which he commended a "noble diction" that evoked "dignity and elevation." Nobody in more than two thousand years since then has better described the timbre a journalist should seek, a rhetoric that is as accessible as everyday speech and yet subtly more formal and refined.

George Orwell made the same essential argument in his 1946 essay, "Politics and the English Language," one you should read in its entirety and take to heart. As the title implies, Orwell saw the battle for precise, meaningful language as one closely related to his political stances against fascism, communism, and imperial capitalism. When language failed, when euphemisms replaced concrete words, truth itself was sacrificed. What is most bracing in Orwell's defense of the written word is the sheer common sense of it. He decries "pretentious diction," "meaningless words," "dying metaphors," "staleness of imagery," the entire "catalogue of swindles and perversions." He offers a list of six rules, such as avoiding jargon, self-editing stringently, and using active rather than passive voice.

How often do you see a lazy writer echo the popular argot of the moment? How many leads have you read lately that parrot the phrase "perfect storm"? (In my time, the equivalent was the mantra from the movie *Network*, "mad as hell and not gonna take it anymore.") Phrases that initially conveyed meaning become, through thoughtless repetition, mere clichés; think of "politically correct" or "counter-intuitive." As for tone, here is a scene from Pete Hamill's memoir *A Drinking Life*. During his tryout as a reporter for the *New York Post*, Hamill covers the eviction of a Brooklyn family. The city editor, Paul Sann, calls him over for a critique.

> Not bad, he said.
> Thanks.
> I like the part about the rain falling down his face.
> Thanks . . .
> He lit a Camel. Then he pointed at a paragraph near the end.
> You see this, he said, where you say this is a tragedy?
> Yeah.
> I'm taking it out. And don't you ever use the fucking word "tragedy" again. You tell what happened, and let the *reader* say it's a tragedy. If you're crying, the reader won't.

In his own way, Sann was expressing the cardinal rule of feature-writing: Show, don't tell. When I have taught this precept to my classes over the years, I've often used two songs by Joni Mitchell to demonstrate the difference between showing and telling. (Forgive me for being so sixties; I promise not to hold class on the lawn.) These two songs, "For Free" and "Furry Sings the Blues," tell essentially the same story. A pop-music star, ambivalent about her riches and fame, encounters a gifted, obscure musician. In the case of "For Free," the musician is a nameless streetcorner busker; in "Furry Sings the Blues," it is an actual Memphis bluesman, Furry Lewis. Now look at how Mitchell *tells* in the first song and *shows* in the second.

I slept last night in a good hotel
I went shopping today for jewels
The wind rushed around in the dirty town
And the children let out from the schools
I was standing on a noisy corner
Waiting for the walking green
Across the street he stood
And he played real good
On his clarinet, for free.

Old Beale Street is coming down
Sweeties' Snack Bar, boarded up now
And Egles The Tailor and the Shine Boy's gone
Faded out with ragtime blues
Handy's cast in bronze
And he's standing in a little park
With a trumpet in his hand
Like he's listening back to the good old bands
And the click of high-heeled shoes
Old Furry sings the blues
Propped up in his bed
With his dentures and his leg removed

"For Free" never gets past its single, self-pitying in-sight: *Gee whiz, I wish I could be virtuous and penniless again.* Both Mitchell and the street musician are one-dimensional. They never change; they never interact; they just are. "Furry Sings the Blues," in contrast, un-folds detail by detail, action by action, just like a care-fully reported, finely wrought work of journalistic prose. Mitchell and her entourage provide the "drink and smoke," and in return Furry provides the music, "mostly muttering" and "sideshow spiel," but occasionally gripping. At the pivotal moment of the encounter, he "points a bony finger" at Mitchell and says, "I don't like you," as everyone nervously laughs, pretending it was just "the old man's standard joke." With all this showing, Mitchell earns the epiphany of her final verse:

Why should I expect that old guy to give it to me true
Fallen to hard luck
And time and other thieves
While our limo is shining on his shanty street

You would be entitled to ask how all this comes back to journalism. One of the greatest snares for a young writer is emotion, whether the emotion of guilt Mitchell expressed in those songs or the emotion of compassion Pete Hamill meant to convey with the word "tragedy." When you show instead of tell, when you write with nouns and verbs, when you put your faith in the concrete and in the reader's ability to comprehend it, you will own emotion instead of emotion owning you.

One of my Columbia students in the mid-1990s was Chris Chivers, a Marine veteran of the first Gulf war. Maybe the military experience has something to do with Chris's ability to stay calm in treacherous situations. Maybe he acquired a heightened appreciation of words because his father, a Vietnam veteran, came back from that war to unplug the family TV forever. In any event, Chris was hired by *The New York Times* a few years out of Columbia and in 2004 was assigned to the Moscow bureau. Barely two months into his stint there, he went to the city of Beslan, where Chechnyan terrorists had taken hostage a school full of children. He was there as the stalemate erupted into violence. His report, far from giving in to emotion, far from telling the reader what to feel, packs an almost unbearable power into acutely observed details conveyed in precise, accessible language. Here are the emblematic passages:

> When the first tremendous explosion shook the air, sending a blast wave through the neighborhood around Middle School No. 1, the crowd of women near the southern police barricades buckled over. An old woman's eyes welled instantly with tears. She began to pound her head with her fists. Another woman wailed.
>
> "Nayyyyyyyyyy!" she screamed, and collapsed to her knees.

> In the beginning the volume of fire was unrelenting. But within minutes there came a brief lull, and a white Volga raced along parallel to the police lines, its engine high-pitched and complaining as it weaved down the road as fast as it could go.
>
> When it passed a crowd that had sought cover behind a thick brick wall, a child's face could be seen, that of a dirty shirtless boy who sat crying on the lap of a man who held him in a tight embrace. The car raced past. The crowd traded news.

"Children made it out!" someone said, and the word was passed along.

More cars sped toward the group, a column of makeshift ambulances, some crammed with four, five and six children. Many children were stripped to their underwear, looking filthy. Some sat upright and calm. The eyes of others were jumpy with fright. A few drank from water bottles with trembling hands. A van pulled up with a man whose left eye was blackened shut, blood running in a rivulet along the side of his face. A skinny boy who looked 14 sat shirtless beside him.

"Where's the hospital?" the driver yelled.

Everyone pointed. "There!" The car lurched away.

The morgue had reached capacity. Children and dead Russian fighters were arranged in rows on the grass.

One row contained 13 dead and bloodied children, aged roughly 4 to 16. The youngest, a boy, shirtless and with his hands folded neatly on his stomach, was unclaimed. A few were covered with sheets or towels, which mothers passing by lifted, to see if they hid the faces of their missing children. One girl, a young teenager in a dress, appeared to have been executed, having been shot through the eye.

The covered remains of one woman, carried
out of the hospital and set in the hospital yard,
told of a terrible end. Her bare feet protruded,
showing soles of feet that were covered with
fresh nicks and cuts, as if before she died, she had
run and run and run.

There is a story in the Talmud of the ancient rabbi
Hillel being challenged to explain the entire Torah while
standing on one leg. "What is hateful to you, do not do
unto your neighbor," he replies. "The rest is commentary. Now go and study." In the same spirit, I would tell
you there is nothing so complex or abstruse about the
precepts of excellent writing. Be clear, be formally correct, show instead of tell. All the rest is execution. Now
go and practice. Once you have mastered the founda-
tions, you can start creating language that is literary and
artistic.

About Books

One summer afternoon in 1987, I typed out my resigna-
tion letter from *The New York Times*. I was thirty-one
and had been on the paper less than seven years. By most
measures, I was throwing away my career. Having
proven myself as a reporter in the Metro and Culture
sections, I was getting feelers from editors about a position in the Washington bureau or perhaps a posting in
West Africa for the Foreign desk. I certainly felt the al-
lure of those opportunities, and I recognized that the

Times was one of the handful of news organizations expansive enough to keep a journalist's curiosity entertained for decades. I also held a deep personal loyalty to the top editors, Arthur Gelb and the recently retired A.M. Rosenthal, who had taken me from the obscurity of suburban Chicago to the Xanadu of West 43rd Street.

Against all those emotions, though, I burned with the desire to write books. As much as I had adored the *Times*, what I craved more than a prestigious assignment was the maximum possible control over what I wrote and how I wrote it. It seemed to me that every article I had ever done fell into one of two categories. Either I had enough space to say what I wanted but not enough reporting time to know what I wanted to say, or I had enough time but not enough space. Now, after false starts on two prospective book topics, I had landed a contract to write about a brilliant, committed teacher and her immigrant students in a high school on New York's Lower East Side. There is a famous aphorism from Oscar Wilde that goes something like, "Be careful what you wish for; you might get it." In getting my wish of a book contract, I was suddenly faced with the question of what made a nonfiction book different from the newspaper and magazine articles I had been writing ever since high school.

More than any of my subsequent books, then, *Small Victories* served as an exercise in much trial and many errors. Of the 220,000 words I submitted in what I thought to be my final draft, I ultimately cut 50,000, the equivalent of several months' labor. As I told you earlier, my credibility comes from my failures as much as from my successes. Out of the arduous process of writing *Small Victories*—at one point, the publisher was so distressed by the bloated manuscript that he threatened to halt payment on my contract—emerged some very firm views about nonfiction narrative.

My first mistake was to believe that with the dimensions of a book I could and should include everything I turned up in my research. I took book length as a license for digression. I was vain; I wanted the world to see the tenacity of my research, to admire every factoid like a precious gem. I embraced a similar sense of excess in my writing. Freed from a newspaper's constraints on personal style, I reverted back to all the worst habits of my callow youth—the strained metaphors, the emotional tone, the pursuit of punchlines at the expense of story. I wanted to leave proof on every page that a Writer was present. I spent the first three chapters of my initial draft, probably 30,000 words in total, in an orgy of self-indulgence. Very interestingly, and I have come to see very typically of first-time authors, the deeper I wrote into the book, the more I began to calm down and trust my material. Nobody could stay in a lather that long.

Far from taking me away from the skills I had developed in daily journalism, book-writing required me to further refine them. Foremost was following the admonition to show instead of tell. In writing for a newspaper or magazine, I could always depend on quoting people, whether recounting events or recalling emotions. In narrative nonfiction, at least the type I produce and admire, all plot, and indeed all meaning, must be embedded in events and actions rather than retrospective commentary. I use direct quotation only in the form of conversation or interior monologue. To reconstruct actions and feelings demands that I gather finer-grained detail and that I assume full responsibility for the accuracy of my depictions. The questions I ask most often in my book research get at the increments of behavior. *And then what happened? And how did that make you feel?* I often envision myself collecting the ceramic chips that will ultimately form a mosaic. My goal, if you'll permit me this one mixed metaphor, is to create what is called in theater the "suspension of disbelief"—the transporting sensation, in this case, that a reader is actually experiencing the events rather than reading about them.

As a fiend for structure, I had to adapt what I knew from daily journalism to the vaster mass of material at my disposal for a book. I had to engineer a narrative that would engross a reader from the outset without giving away anything essential. This meant harnessing chronology without becoming its hostage. A book might well open with a scene that occurs somewhere in the midst of the action. The author James B. Stewart has often spoken about starting with the event that upheaves the existing order, which is another way of saying the moment that establishes the dramatic tension. I call this "murder-mystery structure"; the Greeks called it *en medias res.* One of my favorite nonfiction writers, Melissa Fay Greene, does it brilliantly in her book *The Temple Bombing*, which opens with this account of an attack by white supremacists against an Atlanta congregation whose rabbi is a civil rights advocate:

Fifty sticks of dynamite in the middle of the night blew apart the side wall of the Temple, Atlanta's oldest and richest synagogue, which stood in pillared, domed majesty on a grassy hill above Peachtree Street.

The brick walls flapped upward like sheets on a line. Offices and Sunday school classrooms burst out of the building; the stairwell came unmoored and hung like a rope ladder; bronze plaques commemorating the war dead from the two world wars spun out like saucers; the stained-glass windows snapped outward, like tablecloths shaken after dinner; and all was momentarily red-hot, white-lit, and moving like lava. Then the strangely animate flying rooms and objects stood still—as in the children's game of musical chairs, the children freeze when the music stops—leaving erratic silhouettes and capricious statues of rubble, burst pipes, ashes, and mud, the whole of it colorfully twinkling in the quiet night from the bright bits of stained glass sprinkled over the scene.

By violating chronology, Greene actually allows herself to subscribe to it. Having enticed the reader with this compelling episode, she now has the liberty to go back decades through the social history of Atlanta and then forward in time past the event to the arrest, trial, and acquittal of the accused bomber.

Within any given scene, and within the narrative as a whole, an author should not break out of time sequence unless there is a compelling reason. For me, this was a difficult discipline to acquire. As I wrote my thousand or so words a day, I could not grasp that the amount of plot I might cover in two months might take a reader two hours. I kept flashing forward, making portentous announcements of what would happen or what so-and-so would later realize, just to make sure the reader wouldn't get bored and quit on me. Beyond that, I thought I was being artistic; in reality, I was just depriving my own work of its drama, its capacity to take a reader by surprise. Only with my third book, the first of mine edited by the renowned Alice Mayhew of Simon and Schuster, did I get religion. "Stay in the moment," was Alice's mantra. She did not mean subscribing to a diaristic stringency but being faithful to the overall sense of forward motion in a book.

The challenge is to make a book fulsome without being episodic. A clearly understood theme must govern the choice of what goes on the page and what stays in the notebook. An overarching sense of story must guide your hand. Like me, many newspaper and magazine journalists feel most comfortable building a first book on immersion reporting—essentially being around a central person or place as close to 24/7 as possible—because the methodology is familiar. The risk of such books is to think every observed detail, every overheard conversation, belongs. A work of narrative nonfiction is not a Studs Terkel oral history or a Frederick Wiseman documentary, forms that eschew (or pretend to eschew) editing and selectivity in the interest of achieving greater fidelity. You must shape reality without misshaping it.

My colleague and fellow author Michael Shapiro likes to say that every book has a question beating at its heart. I can see in retrospect how this formulation applies to every book I have written. Will a great teacher quit? Will a minister triumph in a blighted neighborhood? How did the same people who elected Franklin Roosevelt wind up electing Ronald Reagan? Why do Jews, perceived by others as uniquely unified, fight so bitterly among themselves? Who was my mother before she was my mother? Beyond these foundational questions, I have developed a kind of test for each bit of information I consider adding to a manuscript. Does it advance the narrative? Or deepen the portrait of a major character? Or edify the larger subject? If it meets any of those criteria, I include it; if it meets none, I omit it.

Aristotle wrote about all this in *The Art of Poetry*. "A plot does not possess unity, as some people suppose," he argued, "merely because it's about one man." What Aristotle means by unity is, in part, the inexorable quality of selecting only the material that matters. A central character is not merely someone who does things and has things done to him. He must experience "change of fortune," and that change must be "accompanied by a discovery or reversal of both." Aristotle is talking about what makes a page-turner. So I'm a latecomer to enlightenment. It's better than never getting there at all.

Love and Quarantine

In 1869, a newcomer by the name of Samuel Langhorne Clemens rented a room in a local boardinghouse and took the position of managing editor of the *Buffalo Express*. Not quite thirty-five, he had started his journalism career in his teens as an apprentice printer in his native Missouri and sharpened his craft as a reporter on newspapers in Nevada, San Francisco, and Sacramento. Like so many journalists before and since, he also aspired to writing fiction, and he had begun selling short stories six years earlier under the pen name Mark Twain, though another fifteen would pass before his masterpiece, *Huckleberry Finn*, appeared. When Clemens introduced himself to the *Express*'s readers, he made this puckish promise: "I shall always confine myself to the truth except when it is attended by inconvenience."

In his confession of dual loyalties, to fact and to invention, Twain anticipated one of the most thrilling and troublesome aspects of journalism, the interplay between fiction and nonfiction. In certain ways, these two genres should be entwined like lovers, sharing mutual influence. In other respects, they must be quarantined to keep them from being fatally infected by each other. In my own life as author and professor, I have benefited enormously from what fiction has to teach nonfiction. Yet I have also come to despair the increasingly porous line between them, the casual blurring of factuality and fabrication, particularly in works of memoir, family history, and that ever-so-fuzzy category of "literary journalism."

I'm not referring here to the Jayson Blairs and Jack Kelleys who knew full well they were breaking the most fundamental rules of journalism; I'm talking about some very esteemed writers—Vivian Gornick, John Berendt,

Truman Capote, Edmund Morris—who have deviously walked both sides of the street simultaneously. I'm also talking about documentary filmmakers who pass off staged reenactments as archival footage, and reality-TV shows that invent utterly unreal premises, and, for that matter, directors like Oliver Stone who braid together historical events and loony invention. (If you believe Stone's film *JFK*, as much of the unsuspecting public probably did, Lyndon Johnson arranged Kennedy's assassination.) They all claim the power of fact while exercising the creative license of fiction, and the result is to hoodwink the reader or viewer, eroding the very idea, the essential integrity of nonfiction.

I should warn you that there will be few rewards in this life for hewing to a standard of factuality in nonfiction. Yes, daily newspapers have staff copy-editors in part to smoke out falsehoods, and major magazines keep fact-checkers to verify details, descriptions, and the essence, if not the exact wording, of direct quotations. If a reputable news organization discovers one of its journalists has invented material, there will be much breast-beating and self-examination. But the individual perpetrators, as I told you earlier, will profit by their notoriety more than they will suffer. University scholars will tell you that you're naïve to think there is such a thing as a fact. Literary critics will tell you truth can only be achieved through surmise and speculation. Publishing houses will complicitly look the other way while you violate any journalistic or historical norm, if it helps the book sell. If you're lucky, as I've been, you'll write for one of those rare editors who still hew to the classic values. Ultimately, though, you will have to set your own ethics and be prepared to be treated like some bluestocking, some prude, some fool, as a result. I'm telling you, though, you'll be fighting the right fight.

Like any other capitalist, I would love to have my books sell well and bring me lots of filthy lucre. Like any other journalist with artistic ambition, I want my books to read as compellingly as novels. So the question is not one of choosing between the staccato conventions of wire-service journalism and the emotional and aesthetic richness of fiction. The question is knowing what to borrow and what to resist, when to be entwined and when to be quarantined.

When I was on the high-school paper, my adviser introduced me to the work of the New Journalists. That was no accident. Robert W. Stevens was not a journalist by training or temperament; he was a theater teacher and director, an utterly brilliant one who had our high school performing *Hamlet* and *Arms and the Man* instead of the usual musicals. The principal asked him to take over the paper on the correct assumption that a teacher as driven and inspiring as Mr. Stevens could master any challenge. Perhaps because his own inclinations ran toward drama, toward narrative of a kind, Mr. Stevens responded strongly to the journalism of Tom Wolfe, Gail Sheehy, Gay Talese, and Joan Didion. Their collective breakthrough was to demonstrate how the techniques of fiction—dramatic tension, character development, interior life, shifting point-of-view, disordered chronology—could be applied to nonfiction. The ultimate goal was and is to prove that journalism could limn the mysteries of the human condition just as intricately and empathetically as could any novel. One of the few high-school graduation presents that I still have is Wolfe's New Journalism anthology.

In all of my own books, I have sought to marry fictional method to factual material. I think of it as the highest calling in journalism, our claim to a place in the canon, our proof that all literary things are possible without sacrificing a reporter's rigor. Every serious journalist I know reads deeply in fiction, and not only for diversion and vicarious experience. We read fiction, and I hope you will, as an ongoing course in structure, voice, pacing, and the other building blocks of narrative. I remember hearing the acclaimed educator Deborah Meier say that when she was growing up and going to Yankees games with her brother, she went because she wanted to marry Joe DiMaggio, and he went because he was studying how to play the game. Writers, Meier said, need to read books that way, not as spectators but as apprentices.

In the nonfiction seminar I teach at Columbia, a course devoted to developing books, I always assign at least one novel. The most exciting American fiction, at least to my taste, uses a kind of journalistic research to fertilize the fictional imagination, and many of these books have plumbed social issues earlier and better than have the journalists who are supposed to do so every day. I am thinking of what Richard Price did for drug trafficking and racial friction in *Clockers* and *Freedom-land*, what Bharati Mukherjee and Lorraine Adams did in different ways for immigration in *Jasmine* and *Harbor*, what Philip Caputo did for famine, civil war, and relief missions in *Acts of Faith*. If you're willing to indulge me in one aphorism from a Nazi apologist, these books meet Ezra Pound's definition that literature is news that stays news.

The challenge is to accept fiction's influence, to study and apply its narrative means, without ever adopting its poetic license. Fiction and nonfiction, you see, establish very separate contracts with a reader. Nonfiction promises accuracy, to the greatest degree humanly possible, and in return has the power of actuality. No matter how implausible an event or an action, the nonfiction author can fairly say to a reader, *But that's what really happened*. Fiction does not enjoy the escape catch of implausible fact. Fiction promises its readers psychological truth in exchange for the suspension of disbelief. In the Harry Potter series or Stephen King's horror novels, as much as in the naturalistic fiction of Ian McEwan, the freedom to invent carries with it the responsibility that the invention make the deepest kind of sense. A novelist who has to defend his creation by telling a reader, *But that's what really happened*, is a novelist who has failed.

A reader takes the risk of believing the author who claims to write nonfiction. Without a newspaper copy desk or a magazine fact-checker to conduct due diligence, without the voluminous footnotes that specify source materials in scholarly works, every individual journalist decides whether or not to obey the rules. When a nonfiction author mouths the vows and then breaks them, that writer also breaks a fundamental bond with the reader. Like an infidelity in a marriage, one transgression, no matter how momentarily pleasurable, tears apart the fabric of trust forever.

Straddling the line between fiction and nonfiction back in Buffalo, Mark Twain had the self-awareness to joke about crossing it for the sake of mere convenience. The more-or-less nonfiction writers of recent times rarely volunteer such candor. Their crimes have to be discovered by disgruntled sources or investigative reporters, or unwittingly revealed in an impolitic comment, which is, of course, instantly disavowed. Yet the work itself is exactly convenience, convenience and deceit, by some of the lions of nonfiction literature.

One of the books to which Mr. Stevens introduced me was *In Cold Blood* by Truman Capote. I read it with the awe and credulity of my entire generation of journalists, mesmerized by the retelling of murder in a placid Kansas town, completely persuaded by the intricate assembly of detail. I uncritically accepted the legend of the book, which is that Capote possessed such preternatural powers of observation and recall that he never took a note. Something like twenty-five years later, the author and professor Ben Yagoda was foraging through the *New Yorker* archives and discovered the galley proofs of Capote's first chapter, which appeared as an article in the magazine. William Shawn, the editor, wrote in numerous places, "How know? Discuss w/author." Yagoda was never able to find out if those discussions occurred or how Capote's manuscript passed through the fact-checking process. Eventually, though, it became clear that Capote had not relied only on a prodigious memory; he had inserted invented scenes among factual ones. He had run a con game on his readers. Instead of pioneering a new form of journalism, what he dubbed the "non-fiction novel," Capote had shown the path toward fooling the reader and getting away with it.

Given both the artistic and commercial success of *In Cold Blood*, many others have followed his model. One of the phenomena of the book business in the 1990s was John Berendt's *Midnight in the Garden of Good and Evil*, a true-crime yarn populated with a transvestite, a voodoo priestess, an antiques fanatic, and sundry other oddballs of Savannah, Georgia. In addition to selling several million copies, the book very nearly won the Pulitzer Prize, but in the judging process its authenticity began to unravel. Ultimately, Berendt admitted to inventing dialogue, altering chronology, and exaggerating details, all of which for him fell into the realm of "rounding the corners to make a better narrative." The problem is, writing nonfiction means having to reconcile yourself to the corners that refuse to be rounded, the facts you can never know, the informants who died before you got the chance to interview them. The payoff is your reputation, your good name.

In the realm of literary nonfiction, nobody had a much better name than Vivian Gornick. *Fierce Attachments*, an unsentimental memoir of her relationship with her mother, is considered a model of the genre. When Gornick addressed a conference on "creative nonfiction" at Goucher College during the summer of 2003, though, something interesting happened. She talked about how much of her nonfiction she had made up— composite or entirely fictitious characters in her articles for the *Village Voice*, fabricated scenes and conversations in *Fierce Attachments*. One of the students who attended the conference disclosed Gornick's admissions in an article for the webzine *Salon*.

At that time, I knew nothing about the controversy. I was busy doing the research for my own book of family history, a book about the lives of my long-deceased mother and her parents. I had spent a week earlier in the summer in Uruguay, tracking down the story of how a scant few relatives made it safely there from Poland shortly before the rest were exterminated by the Nazis. I had gone to Bangor, Maine, for several days to learn what I could about my grandfather's half-year working in a shoe factory there—the only decent money he made through the entire Depression. I was interviewing my mother's friends, relatives, classmates, old boyfriends. And as I was driving back to Manhattan from my aunt's apartment in Connecticut on the late afternoon of August 5, I switched the car radio to "Fresh Air." In the final segment of the show, the critic and professor Maureen Corrigan spoke about Vivian Gornick's betrayal. She spoke as someone who had read, adored, and often taught *Fierce Attachments*, and at times it sounded to me as if her voice would break. Some of what she said is worth repeating to you now.

Lies don't make an autobiography a lesser work of literature. In the women's autobiography course I teach, we always study the work of Mary McCarthy and Lillian Hellman, each of whom famously accused the other of lying and both of whom told some world-class whoppers. But what lying does do is damage the relationship between reader and memoirist. Autobiography is a genre that is defined solely by a handshake. There's no internal distinction between an autobiographical novel and an autobiography. Rather, it's the autobiographer's pledge to try to tell the truth that makes a reader respond differently. I say try because, as the theorists rightly point out, autobiography is an impossible genre. Time and literary style inevitably distort memories, and the person writing is not the same person who lives the life. But the autobiographer gives his or her word to try, and we readers give our trust. And when this quaint contract turns out to be a con, we feel like rubes.

I wish you vaulting ambition as a writer, and taste, and substance. I wish you the strength, too, to resist those secret compromises against facts, truth, accuracy. When you write a book, you willingly step into the public arena, no longer reporting but being reported upon, no longer jotting down notes on the debate but joining in it. You should welcome the conflict with journalists, scholars, critics, and others who will read your work and challenge your version of reality with their own. That kind of disputation is healthy for a society and it will keep your talents sharp. Never be afraid to defend the vision of the world that you have committed to the page. But make sure you can defend it, because every charlatan in our midst undermines the credibility of us all.

■ Career

In all I've told you so far about temperament, reporting, and writing, I've constructed an ideal journalistic world. It is a world without resumes, rejection letters, boring assignments, newsroom budget cuts, backbiting colleagues, and tyrannical editors. It is a world that does not exist. In becoming a journalist, you are not only acquiring certain skills, developing an aesthetic, and subscribing to a set of ethics. You are managing a career, your own. You are trying to fit all your ambitions and yearnings into the marketplace, into the need to make a living. There is nothing inherently unsavory about the process. Journalists work for themselves, but also for an audience. What we sell is something good and precious, the most incisive and artful rendering of human events that we can produce. If you don't feel that way, then you might as well surrender and apply to law school.

One of the questions I hear most frequently from people your age is whether they have to take journalism courses to get a job. In a way, that inquiry is the beginning of any aspiring journalist's encounter with the real world. My answers are that it depends on which school and what you mean by school. I can trace my own career back to an afternoon in eighth grade. My hometown had just built a new middle school, and so my English teacher, Mr. Powell, decided it ought to have a school newspaper. He put out a call over the intercom for volunteers, and we assembled in his room.

Despite his horn-rim glasses, corduroys, and crewneck sweaters, so Ivy League casual, Mr. Powell could be an intimidating man. He showed visitors home movies of his son's victorious matches on the high-school wrestling team, and he once required me to pronounce the word "brusquely" in front of the entire class. "Bruss Kelly?" he shouted, mimicking my sight-reading of the unfamiliar syllables. "You make it sound like an Irishman." The resulting snickers still echoed in my brain months later, as Mr. Powell bluntly asked all of us quailing volunteers what position we wanted. Somehow I piped out, "Editor in chief." Since nobody else matched my naïve audacity, I wound up overseeing the *Middle School Message*.

So began the consummate educational experience of trial and error. It continued with my high-school paper, the *Highland Fling*. (Not until thirty years after graduating did I realize this referred to a Scottish dance.) I was the awestruck greenhorn writing sports articles in the shadow of the exceedingly cool seniors who ran the show. We had no guidance; we had no tutelage; it being 1969 and 1970, the upperclassmen overwhelmed the inexperienced teacher who was the adviser. Some of what they did was delightful—a satire column that lampooned school events by couching them in Greek and Roman myths—and much of it was inane and self-indulgent. We had a sort of ongoing competition to write the headline with the most alliteration. I still remember this one about a student rock band: "Moonshine's Grapevine Music Fine with Swine's Pagan Pink Ripple Wine." The whole experience was heady and impossibly smug. It never occurred to us to report on much of what was occurring in our school—the deep divides, occasionally turning violent, over race relations and the Vietnam War.

A new principal arrived the following fall, my junior year, and he appointed Mr. Stevens the faculty adviser. Mr. Stevens was all about high standards and looming wrath. We knew as much from his record as director of the school plays. Sometimes I attended the rehearsals just to hear his eloquent eviscerations of faltering actors. There was one boy with a slight lisp who played a minor role in Tennessee Williams's *Summer and Smoke*. One night, his sibilance exhausted Mr. Stevens's patience. "You . . . you . . . you," Mr. Stevens declared, and the entire auditorium grew silent, waiting for the calumny. "You young mailman!" Sure enough, though, the lisp had vanished by opening night. Mr. Stevens was capable of the same explosions as newspaper adviser. He would oversee ruthless postmortems of each issue of the *Fling*, and in my senior year, when I was editor, I objected one time too many. "Sam," he said aridly, "you are a detriment."

As I told you in the last chapter, though, Mr. Stevens exposed us to the most exhilarating journalism of the time. We studied the way real journalists had covered or miscovered real stories. We went to scholastic journalism conferences and competitions. He made us feel we could take on any adult issue. I wrote reviews of Broadway plays. I reported on a speech by Gloria Steinem at nearby Rutgers University. I looked into the effects of New Jersey's decision to lower the legal age of majority from twenty-one to eighteen. Mr. Stevens trusted me enough to let me forge his initials—RWS—on excuse notes when I needed to bring our page proofs to the printer during the school day. I think he even knew that I gave the printers a six-pack at Christmas.

What he provided, in sum, was a concept I mentioned earlier in a different context: freedom within discipline. Mr. Stevens left us free to make the errors of ambition, but not to be sophomoric. If our book reviewer (later to become a published poet) chose to devote his column to William S. Burroughs's *Naked Lunch*, Mr. Stevens did not question such an esoteric choice. If we risked antagonizing the principal by reporting on the unofficial dress code—a photo of a girl with a verboten bare midriff had the caption "Navel Maneuvers"—Mr. Stevens accepted that some of the administrative heat would fall on him. He never saved us from ourselves, and yet he made us want so desperately to meet his expectations. I don't even remember if he was the person who taught me about the inverted-pyramid structure of a news story or the anecdotal lead to a feature. That's the easy part. What I remember is that he taught us to take ourselves seriously, as seriously as the high-school thespians he whipped into a cast for *Hamlet*.

At the risk of being just another middle-aged man awash in nostalgia, I wanted to tell you about Mr. Stevens and the *Fling* because I think my experiences from that time provide an example of how to start learning, which is by doing. If you can do it under the eyes of an inspiring mentor, even better. What I learned in high school made virtually every college journalism class of mine redundant, though by the time I realized that, it made no sense to drop the major. You don't need a class to teach you how to interview or report or construct a basic article if you have the opportunity to work on a high-school or college newspaper (or radio station, television station, or Web site). College should be your time of intellectual exploration, and, in my own case, I despair over every journalism class I took that could have been a class in political science or English literature or virtually anything else.

Fortunately, journalism was not my sole major. I also majored in history and took enough credits for a minor in comparative literature (though Wisconsin did not officially award minors). Although there is little, if anything, of lasting value that I learned in my journalism classes, except for one fine course on First Amendment law, I still draw on much of what I learned in the history and comp lit departments on topics as divergent as twentieth-century China, immigration to America, the barbarian era in Europe, Third World literature, the literature of death and dying. I have forgotten the names of most of my journalism professors; I remember the name of nearly every one from history and comp lit—Schultz, Clovis, Boardman, Archdeacon, Bjornson, Beck—even if a goodly number of the classes met in lecture halls and had more than a hundred students. I remember them because they expanded my brain, opened me up to the wider world, and that is how you should spend your undergraduate years.

I am in no position to judge the quality of every single undergraduate journalism program, and I hold enormous admiration for those professors who combine committed teaching with journalistic productivity and substance. Still, it is a zero-sum game to spend the 120 or 130 credits required for a bachelor's degree. Whenever you choose one class, you are by definition not choosing hundreds of others; when you decide to major in one field, you are simultaneously deciding not to major in others. A journalism program can turn you into a proficient technocrat, someone conversant with the conventions of reporting, writing, and broadcasting, someone able to execute a formula by rote. Most undergraduate programs include, and even require, courses in advertising and public relations, fields that are antithetical to journalism. All too few journalism programs, especially at the undergraduate level, strive to build your cultural and historical literacy and to imbue you with intellectual curiosity. Yet those are the building blocks of journalistic greatness.

If you do insist on majoring in journalism as an undergraduate, then use your reporting skills in selecting the best program. You should beware of journalism departments populated either with communications theorists, all credentials and no practical experience, or with retired reporters and editors, who consider teaching a matter of telling war stories. Look for programs with faculty members who are both brilliant in the classroom and significant in the field. Make sure you will have plenty of one-on-one contact with them, including stringent and detailed line-editing, rather than being passed off to graduate assistants.

Even if you find all those qualities in a journalism department, take a second major, too. Art history, biology, education—anything that will give you content to complement journalism school's craft. Years after my time in Wisconsin, I was pulling out the texts from my urban-history class to help me cover New York City, returning to the novels I had read about death and dying in a comp lit course to help inform my own book about my late mother. A few chapters ago, I was telling you about Manuel Puig's novel *Kiss of the Spider Woman*. I was introduced to Puig, through a different book of his, in yet another literature class. Never did I work so hard for a C-plus.

My experience at Wisconsin left me deeply skeptical about journalism's place in a university, right up until the day in early 1990 when I taught my first class at Columbia. You're probably wondering why, in that case, I agreed to teach, and it's a fair question. In part, I did because I had enjoyed giving a few guest lectures to journalism students over the years. In part, I did because I had just spent a year alone in my apartment every day writing my first book and needed an antidote to cabin fever. And, in part, as I told my students on that initial day, it was up to them to prove to me that journalism actually could be taught and learned in an academic setting. I was the agnostic; they would make me either an atheist or a believer.

The answer is pretty obvious, since I'm still here fifteen years later, much to my own surprise a tenured professor. What, then, changed my mind? That has a lot to do with graduate education in general and also with Columbia as a specific institution, and maybe these answers will help you chart your own path. I cherish Columbia's insistence on putting its student journalists out into the world; they cover the neighborhoods of New York, especially the under-covered ones outside Manhattan. (In my introductory reporting class, I impose what I call the Rule of Brunch: You can't make your beat any neighborhood where you'd be likely to have brunch.) So, at the minimum, seek a journalism program that forces you out of the classroom and the computer lab. Columbia also benefits from having a pass-fail system, because journalism cannot be learned under a system of letter grades. Letter grades work against risk, challenge, and new experience, all of which are essential to developing yourself as a journalist. To the extent you have a choice, to the extent all other factors are equal, look for a journalism program that eschews letter or numerical grades.

The vast majority of my Columbia students did not major in journalism as undergraduates; they majored in art or accounting or geology; many had begun careers as varied as soldier, software engineer, ballerina, real-estate agent, court stenographer, internal-affairs cop, and bartender. Those varied backgrounds enriched them as new journalists and enriched me as their professor/editor. New to the field, they brought a walk-through-fire work ethic and a willingness to fail, understanding that failure is the necessary precondition to success.

Failure liberates you; it liberates you from the fear of failure; it liberates you from the delusion you can somehow be flawless. It is so important for you to realize that. Your generation has been burdened with the pressure to perfect yourselves. You've been sold the false premise that opportunity in America is such a finite resource, such a rare commodity, that if you don't take every A.P. class in high school, if you don't score above 750 on each part of the SAT, if you don't volunteer in a homeless shelter, at least until the college-admission letter arrives, you'll never make it into the Ivy League and your adult life will be ruined. Once in those elite colleges and universities, you'll feel the pressure of applying to law school or business school or med school (whichever your parents insist upon) and scouring the course catalogue for sure As instead of new ideas and stimulating challenges. I remember the one semester I taught undergrads, as a visiting professor at Princeton, and the student who dropped the class halfway through the semester, when it became evident she was headed for a mere B.

Journalism ought to be a refuge from the high-stakes, no-risks version of youth and young adulthood that pervades our country. Yet too many journalists get addicted to approval, the approval they receive from editors or readers or colleagues for endlessly repeating the formulas they long ago mastered. In my years at Columbia, I have had the hardest time reaching those students who had already worked on newspapers or magazines and internalized the accepted style. They could do what I came to disparagingly call the "perfectly acceptable article." To do more than that, though, they had to unlearn before they could learn, and few found the process easy or enjoyable. I would tell them about the way a weight-lifter in training actually rips apart muscle cells in order for them to regenerate stronger. I would tell them about Neil Young and Miles Davis, two of my favorite musicians, not because all of their work excels, but because they never repeated themselves and always took the risk of failing. The students I have most cherished in my years at Columbia are not the most talented but the ones who traveled the greatest distance from the first week to the last.

Standing Your Ground

What I learned about journalism in Wisconsin I learned on the college paper, the *Daily Cardinal*. And what I learned had less to do with skills or techniques than with something perhaps even more valuable—holding on to your principles in a climate of conformity, standing your ground. Every newsroom you inhabit is going to have its unexamined premises, its precious orthodoxies, its craven middle-managers. You will have to find the way to preserve your essential self there. Once you bend your individual talent to suit a party line, any party line, whether a political movement's or a management consultant's, your value as a journalist is gone. You have stopped being a fair broker of information and settled for being a suck-up.

In the Madison I entered in the fall of 1973, and especially around the windowless newsroom of the *Cardi-*

nal, most of us saw being independent as synonymous with being on the Left. We kept a staff riot helmet and marked the Communist conquest of South Vietnam with a front-page banner headline, "VICTORY!!!" Our staff photographer divided his nonjournalistic time between visiting Sandinista revolutionaries in the Nicaraguan jungle and delivering marijuana around town by bike. I spent hours enmeshed in earnest and heated debates about whether our editorial page should endorse the Symbionese Liberation Army's kidnapping of Patty Hearst. In truth, there was little original thought on the *Cardinal*. Our entire ideological spectrum could be summed up by the positions on our basketball team: left guard and far-left guard.

I felt such a desire to go along, because going along meant being accepted, and I was a homesick, homely seventeen-year-old, eager for any foothold in the vastness of the Wisconsin campus. I might very well have gone along with the orthodoxy had I not met one of the *Cardinal's* few genuine dissidents, a fifth-year senior named Jim Podgers. The encounter happened the first week of my freshman year, when I turned in a story about the collapse of a metal float on a lake alongside the campus. With a self-conscious flourish and a nod to Sly Stone, I started the story with a line about "hot fun in the summertime." In the first of many wise line-edits he would provide me, Podgers revised it to "summertime fun."

In addition to caring about politics, rock music, and pot, the socially acceptable interests, I also happened to be a football fan. Sports in general, and football in particular, were signifiers around the *Cardinal*. They meant you were a reactionary, and Podgers was fanatical about football. He seemed to relish his reputation as the staff troglodyte. The *Cardinal* had a bowling league—in Wisconsin, even revolutionaries bowled—and Podgers named his team the Westbook Keglers, a sly allusion to the right-wing columnist Westbook Pegler. His journalistic hero, whom he introduced to my reading list, was Mike Royko, the conscience of blue-collar Chicago. Podgers had a similarly unsentimental worldview. In a newsroom full of utopians, he shot down grandiose visions with the phrase, "'If' took a shit and died." Podgers listened to Bix Beiderbecke, Count Basie, and, most improbably around the *Cardinal*, Frank Sinatra. One afternoon Podgers asked me to walk several blocks from our office to a record store that was holding a particular Sinatra album he had ordered and pick it up for him. I was so mortified that someone might see me in possession of anything so uncool that I bought myself the latest Jethro Tull LP to carry on top. In retrospect, of course, I was like Alfred E. Newman in *MAD* magazine, hiding his copy of the complete works of Shakespeare inside a comic book cover.

A few summers before I enrolled in Madison, an outfit of local radicals had planted a bomb in a university building that conducted military research. The blast managed to kill one physicist, who was against the war. Four alleged bombers went underground. During my freshman year, one of them, Karl Armstrong, was captured and put on trial. His case became a cause célèbre for the *Cardinal*. We regularly ran "Free Karl" editorials and urged readers to rally on his behalf. We exulted in his attorneys' strategy to "put the war on trial," to introduce evidence of American atrocities like the My Lai massacre by way of excusing Armstrong's action. When Armstrong himself finally testified, though, he said all the things his supporters had never said. He expressed remorse, palpable regret, over having taken an innocent man's life. He neither sought nor claimed any moral high ground.

While my *Cardinal* comrades mouthed the rhetoric of class struggle, I was apprenticing in the back-shop alongside a lumberjack's son named Orv Larsen, the genuine blue-collar article. To tell you the truth, I was a lousy assistant. After a few shifts, Orv took me off the press and limited me to collecting and stacking the finished papers in batches of twenty-five. I was also vested with taking a few bucks from him, slipping out to a nearby liquor store, buying him two airline bottles of vodka and a six-pack of beer, and then hiding the booze in the dark, locked room we used for storing photosensitive printing plates. The vodka Orv downed himself. The beers he shared with me and John Burton, a more talented student apprentice. So at two in the morning we would crouch on the cement floor of the plate room, lit only by a deep-red safe-light, and Orv would tell stories. He talked about his Depression childhood in the north woods of Wisconsin, after the lumber industry had moved west, when he and his mother would walk into the county seat with his red wagon to receive their home-relief payment in the form of potatoes. He talked about the printers' union that got busted in during a strike in the Dakotas, the event that made him seethe even then about scabs. In spite of my incompetence on the presses, I had evidently passed some kind of initiation with Orv. As for the rest of the *Cardinal* crowd, Orv said many times, "Get a haircut and be somebody."

My welter of feelings about Podgers, Orv, Karl Armstrong, and the *Cardinal* came to a head during my junior year, when Armstrong's younger brother and fellow fugitive Dwight was captured and put on trial. By that time, I had been elected to the governing board of the paper, which most importantly oversaw financial decisions. Dwight Armstrong's attorneys asked the *Cardinal* to donate five thousand dollars to his defense fund, and the request went before the board. On the night of our vote, the place was packed, with maybe seventy or eighty staff members in the conference room. Every yes vote got applauded, every no vote booed. Mostly the lines broke by who was a student and who was a professor. As I awaited my turn, I could only think about the way Karl Armstrong's supporters had never expressed the slightest regret for the killing of that physicist. I cast my vote against the donation, and it turned out to be the deciding vote. The next time I walked into the *Cardinal* newsroom, the editor called me Shitman Freedman.

The name stuck for quite a while. Eventually, I realized it was a strange sort of compliment.

In Praise of Gradualism

In the autumn of 1982, a revival of Sam Shepard's play *True West* opened in a tiny theater in Greenwich Village and proceeded to cause a major commotion, both at the box office and among critics. The production starred two actors little-known in New York, Gary Sinise and John Malkovich, and had originally been mounted by a nonprofit company operating out of a converted garage in Chicago, the Steppenwolf Theater. Over the next year or two, several more Steppenwolf shows moved to Manhattan—*Balm in Gilead, Orphans, And a Nightingale Sang*—and they introduced such performers as Laurie Metcalf, Terry Kinney, Joan Allen, and John Mahoney. This seeming explosion of talent led to a question in New York theater circles: What was so special and unique about Steppenwolf?

Well, nothing was so unique except this. When Sinise and Malkovich and the rest were finishing up their theater degrees at Illinois State, which ain't exactly Juilliard, they didn't pack their bags for Broadway. They rented a church basement in a Chicago suburb, took day jobs to pay the rent, and gave themselves the opportunity to act and direct all the time. While their starstruck peers in New York were waiting tables and auditioning for TV commercials, the Steppenwolf members were exercising their craft, growing better in increments. They didn't waste their twenties waiting to be discovered, and, paradoxically, they wound up being discovered when their talent was worthy of it.

I've told the story of Steppenwolf to many journalism classes over the years, especially as graduation draws near in the spring, because it offers such a clear lesson about building a journalism career. The most important thing is to be able to write (or broadcast) every day. The important thing, especially in your twenties, is not to be in New York, if that means you're going to wind up as an editorial assistant or a fact-checker, no matter how prestigious or how trendy the news organization. In the fullness of time, if you develop your skills, you'll be able to come to New York, or Los Angeles, or Washington, or Chicago on the strength of those skills. You won't be a supplicant scrambling for any piddling freelance assignments; you'll be a staff reporter or a contributing editor or a producer.

The equivalent of Steppenwolf in my Columbia experience is Craig Laban. Craig entered the journalism school in 1993 as a jazz guitarist and gourmet chef who had done just a slight amount of freelance writing about food. I advised him on his master's thesis—in effect, a very long magazine article or a book chapter—and he delivered the best one I ever have read, a chronicle of the battle between jazz musicians over what constitutes the genre's canon. Photocopies of Craig's final draft were being passed among jazz musicians like underground *samizdat* in the old Soviet Union. A writer on the *Village Voice* even lifted material from it—a compliment, if plagiarism can be considered a perverted form of flattery.

When Craig graduated he had one job offer, and not even from a daily. So he went to the twice-weekly *Packet* in Princeton, New Jersey, and worked a municipal beat, very much as I had decades earlier on the *Courier-News*. After a year or so, Craig's articles caught the attention of the *Philadelphia Inquirer*, which gave him a two-year internship in one of its suburban bureaus, again doing those staples of local government, school board, and crime. From there Craig went on to the *New Orleans*

Times Picayune, and after some time on the metropolitan staff he won appointment as restaurant critic, which in that culinary capital must have been like elevation to Paradise. Ultimately, the *Inquirer* hired him back as its food critic, and he went on to receive the James Beard award as the finest in the nation.

Had Craig insisted, upon leaving Columbia, that he work in a big city and be able to specialize in cuisine, I have no doubt he would have gone jobless until he left the profession. He trusted in gradualism. He trusted that his talent would be found. At risk of sounding Pollyanna-ish about it, I can say that I have never seen a truly gifted young journalist go unrecognized. Maybe in the short run, but never over time. There just isn't that much excellence loose in the world that news executives can afford to ignore it. Your part, though, is to have patience. Your first job won't be the place you'll spend your life; it'll be where you spend maybe eighteen months. So if it's in Pasadena, Texas, or Watertown, New York, or Anniston, Alabama, all places my students have gone, what matters is that you have the chance to work. In those backwaters, you'll have some very esteemed company. J. Anthony Lukas started out on a paper in Harrisburg, Pennsylvania, and Robert A. Caro in New Brunswick, New Jersey.

Few fantasies have as much of a grip on young journalists than that of being a freelance magazine writer. Who wouldn't want the life of a Susan Orlean or a Robert Kaplan—fascinating subjects, exotic places, multiple months for research, thousands of words of space, and finally, display in a major magazine. I have stopped

counting the number of anthologies and writers' conferences devoted to "literary journalism." The problem, I
find myself telling at least several students each year, is
that when you try to make your fantasy into reality you
discover that you are a relatively inexperienced, un-
proven unknown essentially competing for a very finite
amount of magazine ink against the Susan Orlean and
Robert Kaplans of the world. They are the stars, and in
the magazine world, as in Hollywood, stars operate under a different set of rules than everyone else.

The magazine industry sets out in some very specific
ways to exploit the naïveté of young aspirants like you.
To begin with, magazines follow the economic law of
supply and demand with a vengeance. It costs a magazine maybe two hundred fifty or five hundred dollars to
pay a kill fee for an article that would bring the author
five thousand or more if published. So it is in the financial interest of magazines to over-assign on the chance
that for every ten or twenty articles that are rejected
maybe one gets bought. Even if it is bought, an article
passes through several layers of editors, virtually all of
whom want to leave their fingerprints on it, sometimes
by asking for revisions that contradict the instructions of
prior editors. The seemingly endless series of rewrites is
journalism's version of what in the movie industry is
called "turn-around hell."

If your dream is magazine freelancing, then by all
means pursue it. But pursue it wisely. Accept the fact
that, as an actress once told me, "Half of my work is
looking for work." Come up with a strategy for earning
some reliable money so that your food and rent doesn't

depend on the caprice of a magazine editor. Often that means putting yourself in a less glutted market than New York and lining up steady paychecks from uninspiring clients. (I'd also recommend reading the *ASJA Guide to Freelance Writing*, a detailed, practical, and wholly unsentimental collection of advice from successful writers on how to establish and manage your career.)

One of the finest magazine writers I ever taught at Columbia, Ed Leibowitz, moved to Los Angeles straight after graduation to take an unpaid summer internship with *LA Weekly*. It was a calculated gamble, because the weekly's editor was a very accomplished journalist named Kit Rachlis, and Ed mitigated the risk by holding on to his relationship with a trade magazine covering telephone technology. When Ed produced several long features for Kit that summer, he got what is most essential in a freelancing career: a rabbi. Kit went on to edit the Sunday magazine for the *Los Angeles Times*, and Ed went with him as a regular contributor. Eventually, he dropped the phone magazine altogether and started appearing in the *Atlantic* and *The New York Times*.

Mike Sager, whom I wrote about earlier in the book, provides another sensible model. Mike had been on the *Washington Post* for five years—as copy boy, police reporter, night rewrite, and Virginia feature-writer—when he took an unpaid leave in late 1983 to pursue his first assignment from a major magazine. (It was a profile of Vietnam War veterans who stayed on in Thailand, which I mentioned a few chapters ago.) As a known quantity in Washington, Mike also talked himself into contracts with two magazines based in the city, *Regardie's* and the

Washingtonian. With those deals, which came close to matching his final *Post* salary of $28,000 a year, he resigned from the paper. In early 1987, he curtailed his Washington work, took out a home-equity loan, and turned his attentions to the national magazines based in New York. His income dropped so precipitously in a single year that the IRS audited him. Having saved and borrowed to prepare for the lean year, though, Mike could devote the necessary months to reporting, writing, and selling his next two features for *Rolling Stone*, one on pit-bull fights and the other on a high-school narc. They earned him a position as contributing editor, which became the platform for his subsequent career there, at *GQ*, and most recently, at *Esquire*.

The unifying idea in all these case histories—Craig Laban, Ed Leibowitz, Mike Sager, Steppenwolf—is the value, indeed the necessity, of reporting and writing on a daily basis. I cannot promise you that you'll be exhilarated by everything you do on the local paper. I remember how deflated I felt during my first summer on the *Courier-News* when I found out that the Cameron Crowe I was reading in *Rolling Stone* was younger than I was. I remember the Monday nights on the *Suburban Trib* when I was scrambling to report on five different school-board meetings and wondering if this was where my rainbow ended. The *Tribune*, our parent newspaper, would not even let us use the clipping morgue in its Michigan Avenue tower, as if to quash our dreams of someday joining the big time.

I also remember, though, the many compensations of my years in the provinces. They start with the social. I never made closer friendships than in the newsrooms of the *Courier-News* and the *Suburban Trib*. Those places were like the places where you're likely to take your first job—the local paper, TV affiliate, or radio station, the webzine start-up. For all of the satisfaction and prestige I felt at the *Times*, it never felt like home in the way the small papers did. We were in our twenties, most of us, unmarried or wedded but childless. We had nothing compelling in our rented apartments to return to at the workday's end, and so the days were long and intense, and they bled into dance parties, boozy dinners, ball games, bitching sessions. One of our *Suburban Trib* colleagues, Bruce Dold, had been a local legend as a college disk jockey at Northwestern, and a lot of nights wound down with us sprawled, exhausted, and addled in his living room as he spun discs and gave commentary in what we came to call "The Dold Show." If we were consigned to the vanilla districts of suburbia for our work, then we spent our off-hours exploring the edgy and urban—a blues club deep on the South Side; a bar built to midget proportions and owned by several former Munchkins from *The Wizard of Oz;* a Mexican restaurant that served a dish none of us had ever heard of before, raw fish cooked in lime juice, *ceviche*. It was so incredible we each paid the princely sum of thirteen dollars for two helpings apiece, which we washed down with frosty cans of Tecate, another discovery.

We were a bunch of romantics, too, infatuated with journalism and obsessed with any chance to prove ourselves, to break the routine of our local beats. During my one winter on the *Courier-News*, a blizzard roared into

Central Jersey, blanketing the roads. Concerned that if his reporters went home that night they'd never be able to make it back the next morning, when the deadlines hit, our editor, Dave Mazzarella, arranged for the whole staff to be put up at a nearby Holiday Inn. Atop the front page of the next afternoon's paper, Mazzarella inserted the words "SNOW EDITION," the closest thing most of us had ever known to an old-time "EXTRA!!!" We felt like real reporters that day.

We also felt like it when a Syrian immigrant in one of the towns we covered barricaded himself in his home, threatening to set himself afire unless his American-born wife would let him take their children back to the Middle East. The standoff with a SWAT team went on for ten or twelve hours, and in 1979 we were the closest thing to CNN for blanket coverage, with Mazzarella assigning reporters to every facet of the situation. I wrote a sidebar about the two college professors, mentors to the distraught man, who talked him into surrendering. After I filed, I went with my closest newsroom friend, Michael Shapiro, to a bar that made gimlets by the shaker full. Michael had done a profile on the husband for our package of stories. Here was a taste of what the journalistic future just possibly could be. (It certainly was for Dave Mazzarella, who went on to become the editor of *USA Today* and remake the widely disparaged "McPaper" into a reputable and influential publication.)

With twenty-five years of hindsight, I can also tell you that there was a real lasting value to the relentlessly parochial focus of a small newspaper. At the time, I dreaded hearing that phrase from my editors—"the local angle." Now I understand it as a way, however charm-less, of telling us young reporters to figure out how to make a story uniquely and entirely our own, not to merely ape what a larger paper with more resources would do better. The editor of the *Suburban Trib*, Chuck Hayes, had learned this early in his own career in rural downstate Illinois, where he did a muckraking series on the exploitation of migrant labor. Very much in that spirit, he let me spend months reporting, writing, and doing follow-up articles for a series we called "The Hidden Poor," which profiled the pockets of poverty in the wealthy western suburbs of Chicago. Later, I did an investigative series on the Republican political machine in the area—the little-noticed mirror image of Mayor Daley's Democratic juggernaut in Chicago. These series were some of the clips that got me hired by the *Times*.

Actually, though, I think most often now of the story I missed by bucking against the local angle. When I was covering education in the Chicago suburbs, I found out that a local high school had scheduled a fund-raising concert featuring Muddy Waters. It turned out Waters lived in the suburb of Westmont and had a son in the school. So I snatched the opportunity to write a profile of Waters, a biographical survey of his career. When I turned it in, one of my two immediate superiors, John Schmeltzer, wanted to kill it. He told me he didn't know what the piece had to do with our readers. I fumed.

I had admired and learned much from Schmeltzer in doing investigative reporting; once a college wrestler, he now executed take-downs on corrupt politicians, sending at least one to jail. Yet I also made out John to be a hick, what with the baggy suits and that habit of eating a Twinkie in a single bite. By pleading and whining, I did persuade him to run the Muddy Waters article.

Many years later, I realized that, journalistically speaking, John had been the sophisticate and I had been the greenhorn. Had I focused on Muddy Waters not as bluesman but as suburbanite—really, could anything have been more counterintuitive? Did he hold yard sales? Was his wife in the PTA?—I would have had a completely fresh story. Instead, I had settled for doing a third-rate imitation of *Rolling Stone*. Waters didn't even give me an interview.

I'm not suggesting that a small paper can meet every need and every desire. It does not exist to suit your purposes, and if you expect it to do so, you'll wind up prematurely bitter. During my years on the *Suburban Trib*, I looked outside it, too, for opportunities. I wrote record reviews and profiles for the jazz magazine *downbeat*. I sold a couple of long features to the alt-weekly the *Chicago Reader*. I did stringing for *The New York Times* and also did a monthly column about Chicago for a community radio station's listener magazine back in Madison, Wisconsin. I wanted exposure and some extra income, of course, but mostly I wanted to try out different voices, keep taking chances, journalistically cross-train. I was reading fiction all the time, too, discovering the Afrikaner novelist Andre Brink, revisiting the Faulkner works that had confounded me in college.

Meanwhile, a former colleague of mine from the *Courier-News*, Michael Hinds, had hustled his way onto the *Times* by doing a diligent job with a tedious assignment—writing "service" articles for the paper's Home section, such as where to have your smoke-damaged drapes fumigated. "I have the ultimate Michael Hinds story," an editor once told him. "Garage door openers." Well, by the summer of 1981, Michael had earned promotion to covering federal regulatory agencies in Washington, and his editor asked whom he would recommend as a replacement. Michael called me and I thought, what the hell, I'm twenty-five, and if I waste three years writing about smoky drapes and garage-door openers I'll still be mighty young and ready for a better beat. So I told him to put my name in the hopper.

Eventually, I have to tell you, my stringing for the *Times* brought me into a terminal confrontation with Chuck Hayes at the *Suburban Trib*. Without boring you with all the details, I wound up resigning one autumn afternoon in 1981. No two weeks' notice from my end, no severance pay from theirs, I just cleared out my desk that night when the newsroom was empty. I knew the rumor mill would start up early the next morning, so I unplugged my home phone overnight. No sooner did I reconnect it than it rang. On the other end was an editor from the *Times*, asking if I would come east for a job interview with the Home section. I went through about nine of them, trying my hardest to sound knowledgeable and passionate about service pieces while expecting at any moment to be unmasked as a pretender. Finally, I was summoned for my interview with A.M. Rosenthal, the executive editor, the traditional moment for a job to be offered. I'd been tipped off to expect the phrase, "Come, join us."

"I'm not going to hire you as a consumer reporter," Rosenthal said. "You're not a consumer reporter."

I slumped a bit in my seat. My stomach shriveled like a deflating balloon.

"I kept waiting for someone to realize that," I replied. "But I wanted to get on the paper any way I could."

Rosenthal stood at his desk, quickly arranged a fan-tail of papers into a neat pile, as if preparing for his next meeting. I thought about the long drive back to Chicago.

Then he looked at me and said briskly, "You're a news reporter. We'll find you a job in news."

Do What Terrifies You

Feverish with a summer flu, lightheaded from the straight vodka I'd ordered in a foolish effort to impress, I strained to follow the conversation careening around the table in the *Times'* corporate dining room. There was talk about the Nederlanders, who apparently owned a bunch of theaters, and their rivals the Shuberts, except that the Shuberts weren't named Shubert, they were Bernie Jacobs and Gerry Schoenfeld. There was talk about Joe, whom I took to be Papp but didn't dare ask for a clarification. There was talk about ice, which evidently wasn't frozen water but money made by scalping tickets, and about amortization, a word I had never before heard. I should have felt triumphant, seated there with Arthur Gelb, Abe Rosenthal's right hand in editing the *Times,* and the drama critic Frank Rich, and that remarkable culture writer, Michiko Kakutani. Instead, I had premonitions of disaster.

Several days earlier, Arthur had phoned me in the *Times'* bureau in suburban Connecticut, my post since having been hired twenty months earlier, and told me he wanted me to move down to New York, start covering the theater beat. Certainly, I was flattered, because I had worked hard and productively in Connecticut, largely under the tutelage of Jeff Schmalz, most recently reporting on the catastrophic collapse of a bridge on Interstate 95. Apparently that sequence of front-page stories had caught Arthur's eye and brought back a memory of my job interview with him in 1982, when we had talked at length about Eugene O'Neill, one of my favorite playwrights and the subject of a definitive biography by Arthur and his wife Barbara. I should have felt relieved, too, to be summoned to the city. By *Times* rules, I had to live in the region I covered, and I had developed a thorough loathing for Fairfield County with all its horsey-set pretense.

But Arthur was yanking me out of my comfort zone. My entire reporting career up to this point had been spent in the suburbs, and if I had an expertise, it was in exploring and explaining suburbia. As much as I loved going to the theater, how on earth could I ever understand it deeply enough, both as an industry and an art form, to write about it with the authority a reader expected from the *Times*? My first weeks on the beat were filled with blunders. The musical *A Chorus Line* was playing its record-setting 3389th performance on Broadway, a sure front-page story for me. I filed a piece that did not even include a quote from Joe Papp, who had discovered and nurtured the show downtown at the Public Theater. Thank God the culture editor, Bill Honan, spotted my gaffe in the first edition. He snagged Papp at the black-tie dinner celebrating the record and phoned in a comment that I inserted for the later editions. Then I did a feature story on the way theater producers pressured writers to forgo their weekly royalty—a share of box-office income—in order to keep a show financially afloat. I called up Ellen Stewart, founder and doyenne of the LaMama Theater, an Off Off Broadway institution. "Darling," she answered dryly, "we don't pay *anybody* royalties."

Over the months, though, I got less stupid. I found that I genuinely enjoyed learning the intricacies of theater economics, even though I had never covered business before. Any writer would want to interview a star. I actually preferred figuring out, line item by line item, why tickets for the same play cost four or five times more in New York than in London. More generally, I began to appreciate the thrill of climbing the mountain, of mastering the task that had intimidated me. Of the many gifts I received as one of Arthur's protégés, the most enduring is this: *The thing that terrifies you is the thing you must do.* When I teach my book-writing class at Columbia and students tell me of being scared of their project—the scale, the scope, the complexity—I always say that means they've chosen the right topic. For a reporter or producer on a news organization, the lesson would be to force yourself every few years out of your routine, out of what you already know. Be a Trotskyite, a believer in perpetual revolution. What you're rebelling against is your own stasis.

Arthur Gelb never let me rest, journalistically speaking. He was a great pterodactyl of a man, six-foot-four with endless arms, which always seemed to be beating the air as he strode through the newsroom, spewing out brainstorms as he went. The line in the newsroom about Arthur was that he had a million ideas a day and at least one was good. By the time I had grown secure in my reporting on theater, Arthur was hurling me into other kinds of deep water. For a special issue of the *Times* magazine marking the tenth anniversary of the end of the Vietnam War, he assigned me to write about how the war had affected American culture. For another magazine issue, devoted to New York, he assigned me to write about the city's identity as an intellectual capital. I would get maybe three weeks for each of these, and the word from Arthur that rang in my brain was "definitive." I grew accustomed to waking up in the predawn dark, stricken with anxiety. And I grew accustomed to working my way through it.

I should add one caveat here about the chemistry between reporter and editor. It can turn as dysfunctional as any other intense, mutually dependent relationship. Whenever I read about a Jayson Blair or a Stephen Glass or any other plagiarist or fabricator, I am reading about a sociopath, someone like Tom Ripley in Patricia Highsmith's novels, a brilliant, diabolical chameleon. But a chameleon needs a point of reference against which to match its coloration. So I always suspect that beside the chameleon there is an editor with a too-clear, too-exact notion of what an article should be, an editor willing to suspend all the usual ethical norms, all the editorial due-diligence, if a writer can fulfill every preordained expectation. How does that phrase go? *If it's too good to be true, it probably is.*

When I resigned from the *Times* to start on my first book, the hardest thing I had to do was tell Arthur. He had guided so many careers at the *Times*, and I knew he wanted to guide mine, and I could think of no higher compliment. But I told him my departure was his fault. The attributes he had cultivated in me—the appetite for risk and challenge, the ambition to report and write on an ever-larger canvas, even the exposure to so many playwrights and plays—made it inevitable that I would move on. *The New York Times* could offer me incomparable prestige and potential postings literally around the globe, a lifetime of experience. What I craved, what Arthur had taught me to crave, was the freedom to report and write to the limits of my abilities. That and the tingling, stimulating danger of falling on my face.

Failing in Public

I walked into the Borders bookstore just outside Washington early on an Indian summer afternoon in 1996. On the previous Sunday, the *Post* had put a rave review of my book *The Inheritance* on the cover of its book-review section; the critic had even compared it to Tony Lukas's *Common Ground*. For a book about political history, I couldn't have had better exposure in a more appropriate city. Now, as I saw, the Borders store had placed a framed copy of the review and a stack of books next to the cash register, the ideal location. So I went over to introduce myself to the manager and asked her how many copies *The Inheritance* had sold. She logged onto her computer, typed, and clicked. I watched her face drain of color. "None," she informed me.

I spent the rest of that day in a state of suspended animation, not speaking a word to the escort who was responsible for driving me to a few interviews, and I went through those interviews with false cheer and pretend eloquence. In fact, I spent most of the next two years in a condition of similar devastation. I had bet all of my chips on *The Inheritance*. After producing two well-received books of immersion reporting, *Small Victories* and *Upon This Rock*, I had committed myself to something much larger, a political history of twentieth-century America as lived by three generations of three families. For more than four years of research and writing, I had turned down virtually every other writing assignment I was offered, not wanting to deviate for a day from my opus. When the book came out, it received more and better reviews than even the first two—covers in the book-review sections of the *Times*, the *Post*, the *Philadelphia Inquirer*, the *Boston Globe*.

Except that nobody bought it. Well, to be precise, six thousand people did. Every day for months upon months, I would check my answering machines at Columbia and in my home-office, praying for something to reverse the tide. I had just finished teaching my book-writing class on the Monday afternoon in April 1997 when the Pulitzer Prizes were announced. I knew I hadn't won, because winners almost always are tipped off. So out of self-flagellating curiosity, I walked into the room at Columbia where the results had been released. By now, all the reporters had left to file. The floor was covered with discarded copies of the press release. I picked one up and looked at General Nonfiction, my category. I was listed as one of two runners-up. I knew, in that second, the meaning of psychological torture.

I hadn't expected or needed a best-seller with *The Inheritance*. I just could not fathom its irrelevance. It had disappeared. It had sunk without leaving a ripple. Four years of effort had brought me right up to the edge of success, the Promised Land of the Pulitzer in sight just across the Jordan, and it had been denied me. In the aftermath, I thought very seriously about giving up writing altogether. I spoke with a couple of editors about how I might become a book editor instead. I had cynical fantasies of selling myself to rich Manhattan families to ghost-write college application essays for their cosseted children. When I taught my book-writing class each week, when I looked into the attentive, receptive, respectful eyes of my students, I thought to myself, *Why the hell are they listening to me? Don't they know I'm a failure?*

Without my wife and children to keep me grounded in domestic routine, I truly don't know what path I might have taken. I gradually resumed some freelance writing, telling myself mordantly that my goal was to be the most productive depressive ever. My book editor, Alice Mayhew, made sure I didn't slide off the edge of the earth. She would invite me to breakfast or lunch every few months, and my regard for her was so high that I didn't dare indulge in self-pity. I was too afraid she'd never publish me again. As it was, Simon and Schuster had lost several hundred thousand dollars on *The Inheritance*. It was Alice who never stopped believing, even as I flitted through dozens of ideas for a new book, abandoning every one. It was she who encouraged me to push ahead with one about the conflicts within American Jewry, and only after nearly two years of work on it did I finally accept that I had made the right choice. I think it just took me that long to pull myself off the floor.

I'm telling you all this because to be a journalist is to live a public life, with public success and public failure, all of it deeply, inescapably personal. Yes, you can be cushioned to an extent by the reputation of your employer, by the box in which your work is wrapped. Finally, though, it is your words or your voice or your film that is out there. Sometimes the terrible frustration of journalism is not knowing whether you had any effect or not. Sometimes the frustration is knowing all too acutely that the world has rejected your words, the way I found out that afternoon in Borders. Sometimes the frustration is feeling unrecognized, trapped, stymied, stifled, the way I often did at the *Courier-News* and the *Suburban Trib*. Journalists drink to celebrate, and they drink to blunt the pain and frustration, too.

Journalism is a business of proving yourself anew every single story, every single day. Yesterday's scoop is tomorrow's recycling bundle. When I was on the *Courier-News*, I got to cover the musical wake for a member of the band Parliament-Funkadelic who had died in his twenties of leukemia. I stayed up all night for the memorial jam session in a local club and wrote my article, overtired and electrified, for our early-morning deadline. It made the front page. When I returned to the office ten hours later for my regular night shift, I found a note of congratulations from one famously stoic editor. Somehow, over the next day or two, I mislaid it, and I asked the editor if he had a copy. Which he didn't. "In our business," he told me coolly, "praise is evanescent."

So be ready for some tough times, even some bleak times. If you care about journalism and you care about excellence, you cannot help but feel despair when it or you don't measure up. None of us are in this for the money or the acclaim. We know that the friends who went to law school or business school will be richer, and that the ones who went to med school will be both richer and more revered. And, let's face it, when you look around at the newsroom layoffs, at the declining rates of newspaper readership, at the falling ratings for network news, you start to appreciate what an autoworker in Detroit must have felt like circa 1982. Just remember this. When I was on the *Suburban Trib*, one of my oldest friends passed through on his way from law school in Oregon to visit his family in New Jersey. Over pizza and beer, a bunch of us reporters were kvetching about our editors, our beats, all the usual subjects. Back at my apartment later, my friend said, "You guys just don't understand. You expect to like your jobs. Ninety-nine percent of the people I know hate what they do. You don't know how lucky you are."

Epilogue: Ancestor Worship

During the years I spent researching a book on a black church, I traveled with the pastor to Ghana. We went up from the capital of Accra to a small village called Asafo, where the church had endowed a school and medical clinic. One night the conversation between the pastor and the village chief turned to the subject of ancestor worship. How can you be a Christian, the pastor asked, and still worship ancestors? The chief answered that Americans don't understand the meaning of ancestor worship. We don't worship the ancestors instead of God; we worship ancestors as the intermediaries between ourselves and God.

On a Monday morning in December 2004, I engaged in the journalistic version of ancestor worship. I attended a memorial for a longtime *New York Times* reporter named Murray Schumach, who had died several weeks earlier. I did not know Murray—he had retired from the paper about the time I was hired—but we had many friends in common. One of them, Arthur Gelb, asked if I could arrange to have Murray's service held in the World Room at Columbia Journalism School, a fitting place, the home of the original stained-glass window from the newsroom of Joseph Pulitzer's paper, the *New York World*.

As I looked down the rows of chairs on the morning of the service, I saw so many of the journalists whom I had learned from and admired—Arthur Gelb, Anna Quindlen, Gay Talese, and Sydney Schanberg, among others. As they remembered Murray, they inevitably spoke of our shared profession, our common passion. I pulled a pen from my coat pocket and started to jot down what they said.

Arthur Gelb: "Don't be in a hurry to be a star. . . . When you get discouraged, remember that it took me seven years to get my first byline. . . . Talk to the rabbi and the priest. Ask people if their garbage gets picked up on time."

Anna Quindlen: "Murray made the small lives of New Yorkers seem big, because he didn't think of them as small, and he didn't treat them that way."

Gay Talese: "We should be more than courteous with those with whom we sincerely disagree. . . . We must have sensitivity to one's surroundings and empathy for the outsider."

Sydney Schanberg: "The lesson is that we are part of a continuum. We didn't invent reporting. It was passed on to us."

In the year following Murray Schumach's memorial service, I turned fifty. I have been working as a professional journalist now for thirty years, since that summer evening I started my first internship on the *Courier-*

News. I have come to realize, with no small frustration, that I may never achieve the greatness I have sought. There are days, pitching a story to an editor half my age, when I feel like Willy Loman, flailing against his imminent irrelevance. There are days when I think my headstone should read "STILL WAITING FOR HIS BIG BREAK."

Yet I have never stopped loving the work. I have more ideas for education columns for the *Times* than I have columns to fill. I have enough ideas for books to last me into my seventies. Every time I start to write, even if it is just putting my name and a slug on the top of a story, I feel an almost physical sensation of well-being move from my fingertips up through my arms and into my torso, like some writer's version of the fabled "runner's high." It is not that I expect the work to go easily, only that I know I am doing what I was put on earth to do.

If you feel the same way, I hope we'll meet some day. The most selfless pleasure of all is the pleasure of a mentor watching a protégé blossom and flourish. It is what Mr. Stevens, my high-school teacher, felt when I made it onto the *Times.* It is what I feel when one of my Columbia graduates lands a front-page story, wins an award, writes a book. If my words in these pages can help you reach your own dreams, then something indeed will have been passed on.

Works Cited in This Book

Books and Articles

Adams, Lorraine. *Harbor*. New York: Knopf, 2004.

Banks, Russell. *Continental Drift*. New York: Harper and Row, 1985.

Berendt, John. *Midnight in the Garden of Good and Evil: A Savannah Story*. New York: Random House, 1994.

Beresford, David. "Dogged by Haunting Images." *Guardian* (London). August 22, 1994.

Bollinger, Lee. "The Value and Responsibilities of Academic Freedom." *Columbia* magazine. Spring 2005.

Brennock, Mark. "Staring Coolly into Hell." *Irish Times*. April 22, 1999.

Breslin, Jimmy. "The Breslin Report, Honors at Gravesite." *Newsday*. November 22, 1988. (Reprint of original *Herald Tribune* article from November 1963.)

Cahill, Thomas. *How the Irish Saved Civilization: The Untold Story of Ireland's Heroic Role from the Fall of Rome to the Rise of Medieval Europe*. New York: Doubleday, 1995.

Capote, Truman. *In Cold Blood*. New York: Random House, 1965.

Chivers, C.J. "An Agonizing Vigil Leads to Reunion or Despair." *New York Times*. September 3, 2004.

Classical Literary Criticism: Aristotle/Horace/Longinus. London: Penguin, 1965.

Corrigan, Maureen. Commentary on "Fresh Air." August 5, 2003.

Dowd, Tom. "He Played with Feathers." From liner notes to *The Heavyweight Champion: John Coltrane, the Complete Atlantic Recordings*. Rhino/Atlantic, 1995.

Dufresne, Marcel. "Midnight in the Garden of Fact and Fiction." *Fulton County Daily Report*. August 21, 1998.

Fass, Horst, and Marianne Fulton. "The Bigger Picture: Nik Ut recalls the Events of June 8, 1972," www.digitaljournalist.org/issue0008/ng2.htm.

Gavin, Thomas. "The Truth Beyond Facts: Journalism and Literature." *Georgia Review* 45, no. 1, Spring 1991.

Gonzalez, David. "Strong New York Ties Bind Families in Grief." *New York Times*. November 14, 2001.

Gornick, Vivian. *Fierce Attachments*. New York: Farrar, Straus and Giroux, 1987.

Gourevitch, Philip. *We Wish to Inform You That Tomorrow We Will Be Killed with Our Families: Stories from Rwanda*. New York: Farrar, Straus and Giroux, 1998.

Greene, Melissa Fay. *The Temple Bombing*. New York: Addison Wesley, 1996.

Hamill, Pete. *A Drinking Life*. New York: Little, Brown, 1994.

Harper, Timothy, ed. *The ASJA Guide to Freelance Writing: A Professional Guide to the Business, for Nonfiction Writers of All Experience Levels*. New York: St. Martin's Griffin, 2003.

Kakutani, Michiko. *The Poet at the Piano: Portraits of Writers, Filmmakers, Playwrights, and Other Artists at Work.* New York: Times Books, 1988.

Kotlowitz, Alex. *There Are No Children Here: The Story of Two Boys Growing Up in the Other America.* New York: Doubleday, 1991.

Lemann, Nicholas. "Ordinary People & Extraordinary Journalism." *Columbia Journalism Review.* November-December 1991.

Lippmann, Walter. *Liberty and the News.* New York: Harcourt, Brace and Howe, 1920.

Lukas, J. Anthony. *Common Ground: A Turbulent Decade in the Lives of Three American Families.* New York: Knopf, 1985.

Magida, Arthur J. "Probing the Nether World of a Jew Accused of Nazi Crimes." *Baltimore Jewish Times.* June 12, 1987.

Malcolm, Janet. *The Journalist and the Murderer.* New York: Knopf, 1990.

McFadden, Robert D. "After a Dry Summer, Listen to the Rhythm!" *New York Times.* September 18, 1995.

_____. "296 Arrested as Police Raid Cockfight in Bronx." *New York Times.* March 27, 1995.

_____. "Water Main Ruptures, Creating a Huge Sinkhole on Fifth Avenue." *New York Times.* January 3, 1998.

McLean, Bethany. "Is Enron Overpriced?" *Fortune.* March 5, 2001.

Mukherjee, Bharati. *Jasmine.* New York: Grove, 1989.

Orwell, George. "Politics and the English Language." First published in *Horizon* (London). April 1946.

Packer, George. *The Assassins' Gate: America in Iraq.* New York: Farrar, Straus and Giroux, 2005.

Pew Research Center for the People and the Press. *Trends 2005.* Washington, D.C.: Pew Research Center, 2005.

Picasso: Une Nouvelle Dation. Paris: Editions de la Reunion des musées nationaux, 1990.

Price, Richard. *Clockers.* Boston: Houghton Mifflin, 1992.

_____. *Freedomland.* New York: Broadway, 1998.

Puig, Manuel. *Kiss of the Spider Woman.* New York: Knopf, 1979.

Rosenblatt, Gary. "A Cautionary Tale from the Church." *New York Jewish Week.* February 15, 2005.

_____. "Lessons from the Lanner Case." *New York Jewish Week.* July 7, 2000.

_____. "Stolen Innocence." *New York Jewish Week.* June 23, 2000.

Sager, Mike. *Scary Monsters and Super Freaks: Stories of Sex, Drugs, Rock 'n' Roll and Murder.* New York: Thunder's Mouth, 2003.

Schmalz, Jeff. "Covering AIDS and Living It: A Reporter's Testimony." *New York Times.* December 20, 1992.

Schudson, Michael. *Discovering the News: A Social History of American Newspapers.* New York: Basic, 1978.

Schwartzman, Myron. *Romare Bearden: His Life and Art.* New York: Harry N. Abrams, 1990.

Sheridan, Kerry. *Bagpipe Brothers: The FDNY Band's True Story of Tragedy, Mourning, and Recovery.* New Brunswick, N.J.: Rutgers University Press, 2004.

Sterling, Terry Greene. "Confessions of a Memoirist." *Salon.* August 1, 2003.

Talese, Gay. *The Gay Talese Reader: Portraits & Encounters.* New York: Walker and Company, 2003.

Winerip, Michael. "Looking for an 11 O'Clock Fix." *New York Times Magazine.* January 11, 1998.

Wolfe, Tom. *The New Journalism.* New York: Harper and Row, 1973.

_____. "Stalking the Billion-Footed Beast." *Harper's*. November 1989.

Woodward, Bob. *The Secret Man*. New York: Simon and Schuster, 2005.

Woodward, Bob, and Carl Bernstein. *All the President's Men*. New York: Simon and Schuster, 1974.

Yagoda, Ben. "In Cold Facts, Some Books Falter." *New York Times*. March 15, 1998.

Documentaries and Feature Films

Local News, directed by David Van Taylor. Lumiere Productions and Thirteen/WNET New York, 2001.

The Year of Living Dangerously, directed by Peter Weir. MGM, 1983.

Plays

Greenberg, Richard. *Eastern Standard*. Originally produced by Seattle Repertory, 1988.

Hare, David. *Via Dolorosa*. Originally produced by the Royal Court Theater, 1998.

Smith, Anna Deveare. *Twilight: Los Angeles, 1992*. Originally produced by the Mark Taper Forum, 1993.

▄ Index